Cocina Tropical
Jose Santaella

COCINA TROPICAL

THE CLASSIC & CONTEMPORARY
FLAVORS OF PUERTO RICO

JOSE SANTAELLA

FOREWORD BY ERIC RIPERT
PHOTOGRAPHY BY BEN FINK
WRITTEN WITH ANGIE MOSIER

RIZZOLI
NEW YORK

New York · Paris · London · Milan

First published in the United States of America in 2014
by Rizzoli International Publications, Inc.
300 Park Avenue South
New York, NY 10010
www.rizzoliusa.com

2015 2016 2017 / 10 9 8 7 6 5 4 3 2

Distributed in the U.S. trade by Random House, New York

Printed in China

ISBN-13: 978-0-7893-2743-7

Library of Congress Control Number: 2014939021

To my beautiful island,
Puerto Rico, and
its wonderful people.

CONTENTS

FOREWORD

—Eric Ripert

The first time I visited Puerto Rico was 25 years ago. I was invited by my great friend Alfredo Ayala, whom I had met while I was working in the kitchen of Joël Robuchon where Alfredo was training. Six months later, I found myself in San Juan and spent the duration of my three-week vacation immersing myself in the culture, food, customs, landscape, and gorgeous beaches of this jewel of an island.

It's no surprise that during this first of what was to become many trips, I met Jose Santaella at a party. Puerto Ricans love and celebrate life as much as they can and do so through music, dancing, drinking, and eating good food. Jose was no exception—a lover of life, a gourmand, a passionate cook. Years have passed since then and Jose has accomplished so much. He has traveled the world and trained in great kitchens, including a stay at Le Bernardin where I had the great opportunity to work alongside him. I still visit the island every year to see Jose, Alfredo, and all my friends. When I'm there with them I become Puerto Rican all over again.

When I learned about the opening of Santaella restaurant next to the traditional market of San Juan, I was excited about how Jose was evolving *cocina criolla y casera*. This book speaks to that progression. Influenced by the many different cultures that have left a strong imprint on the island, including those of Spain and Africa, Puerto Rican cuisine is a rich and hearty one. Reading the recipes in this book brings back memories of experiencing the bounties of Puerto Rico. I've had so many great times accompanied by *alcapurrias, lechón,* empanadas, *morcilla,* pique, *escabeche,* and *bacalao.* Rice and beans aren't just a staple, but an art form when cooked with knowledge, passion, and love. That's exactly what Jose is sharing with us throughout these pages. This collection of personal, local, and iconic recipes makes me smile and immediately transports me back to the magical island. I'm inspired to try the *pastelón,* the *fricassee de cabrito,* and the *asopao de pollo* in my own kitchen. This book brings Puerto Rico into my home in New York and gives me the perfect excuse to bring my family and friends together, to fill the space with salsa music, to dance, to eat, to laugh, and to once again enjoy all the simple pleasures that life offers us.

Previous: Glistening bottles of pique for sale at a roadside market.
Opposite: Fresh coconuts cut for drinking straight from the shell offer a refreshing treat while shopping at the Farmer's Market in Old San Juan.

The enchantment of the island of Puerto Rico, my home, originates from a source much deeper than the beautiful blue skies, crystal waters and white sand beaches, the rainforest, rolling countryside, and green mountains of the place itself. There is an underlying current here of rich complexity that begins with the indigenous people who first populated the land and runs throughout its history, stirring up the beautiful mix of diverse cultures that make Puerto Rico what it is today. The elements that have come together to create our modern lifestyle are reflected in our love of nature, music, tradition, and food.

Compiling recollections and recipes for *Cocina Tropical* has proven to be much more than just writing down ingredients and cooking instructions. The experience has strengthened my relationship with this island and its *comida criolla*—the food of my place. The story of why this food plays such a large part in my life and work not only is a documentation of my own journey, but also the history of my family and home and of all of those who have helped me along the way.

I was born and raised in San Juan, Puerto Rico's capital city and the entry point for most tourists who visit the island. It's a bustling town—the sparkling metropolis and historic Old San Juan—that is edged by the beaches of the Atlantic Ocean. I had a joyful childhood and grew up with a family who occupied and enjoyed the modern city life but had one foot planted in the rural lifestyles of our grandparents. The result is a diverse reality and exposure to the varied influences that make up the *Isla del Encanto*, or Island of Enchantment. Puerto Ricans are addicted to beautiful, lively cultural traditions and experiences—and those always include celebrations around the table. It is the love of all of these things that led me to pursue a career in food.

Great things happen in and around the Puerto Rican table and the *cocina tropical*—whether in a home kitchen or in a restaurant. I'm lucky to have grown up with both a mother and a father who really enjoyed cooking. They had different specialties and styles, but they each encouraged me to explore taste and experience in my own ways. My grandparents also cooked quite often, and because they were from a different era and grew up in contrasting areas of Puerto Rico, their influence and manner offered me an alternate view of the island. My father worked in the food industry and owned several restaurants. They were not fancy establishments but rather simple places—a pizzeria and cafeterias that offered casual dining opportunities. I spent my days after school stopping in at my dad's restaurants, and knew the patrons and service staff alike. It was a fantastic way to learn that the business of food is multifaceted and touches the community by way of comfort and necessity.

I suppose I always knew that I wanted to be a chef, and when as a young man I took a job working in the restaurant of a noted Puerto Rican chef I knew that I was on my way. The restaurant was Ali Oli, and the chef was Alfredo Ayala. Alfredo is an innovator and was responsible for taking many of our traditional recipes and presenting them in a new, sophisticated light that has allowed us to taste our food as it was and as it could be. Preparing local food in an exciting, modern way was compelling to me, and with him as my mentor I wanted to learn as much as I possibly could. Alfredo saw in me a passion for the business and urged me to travel a bit to broaden my horizons. He encouraged me to learn all that I could while I had the youthful energy to absorb wisdom and technique from other chefs.

Numerous chefs who visited Puerto Rico would come to visit Alfredo at Ali Oli, not just to eat but also to work and learn the nuances of our cuisine. One of those chefs was Alfredo's friend, Eric Ripert (who graciously wrote the foreword to this book). Eric and I became friends, and when I mentioned to him that I would like to move to New York and experience the work going on in his restaurant, Le Bernardin, he made it happen. At the time, Executive Chef Gilbert Le Coze was leading a talented team with Eric as chef de cuisine. Their way with seafood—their dedication to making the fish the star of

the plate and elevating a fantastic ingredient—transformed my perspective. It was an essential time of learning for me in a restaurant with a serious brigade-style kitchen.

While happy to be learning in a different environment, I was hungry for more and decided to move to San Francisco to see what was happening with food on the West Coast. I met Chef Gary Danko there when he led the Dining Room at the Ritz-Carlton, San Francisco. We hit it off immediately, and I began working with him in the restaurant, where I witnessed firsthand what is so special about "California cuisine." Gary was a great teacher, and through his influence I became excited about the prospect of presenting the foods of my home in a similar fashion. I've always been attracted to the art of presenting delicious food, sourced from the finest purveyors, in a way that transports a diner.

Perhaps no other chef has transported us farther into the stratosphere of what can be than Ferran Adrià, of elBulli in Spain. Roberto Enrich, a mutual friend from Barcelona, introduced me to Chef Adrià, and I was fortunate to land a coveted stage position at elBulli. I relished the opportunity to witness and learn some of the otherworldly steps that the elBulli team takes in their unique approach to fine dining and the molecular cooking revolution. I'm grateful to Ferran Adrià for the experience that he shared with such wisdom and caring. Being there as well as traveling to Spain exposed me to the beauty and possibilities that exist when you are rooted in an old culture but excited about the future.

For me, that future was to return to my home, explore the traditional foods of Puerto Rico in a deeper way, and enthusiastically offer my own approach to *comida criolla*. I put together a team of cooks and servers and began working as a caterer—first for small, in-home gatherings and soon for grand parties with gorgeous presentation and sophisticated flavors. Over many years we have catered parties for famous locals and international superstars, but the draw of having my own restaurant—a space to invite friends and strangers alike to experience my cuisine—was so strong and I couldn't ignore the pull. My restaurant, Santaella, opened in June 2011. My goal is for guests to feel they're coming into my home while also spending a luxurious night on the town. The food is elegant but familiar, and our interiors and dining room hospitality reflect my personal style and how I translate "my" Puerto Rico. My friend the architect Jose Toro was instrumental in developing this style. Located across from the thriving market in La Placita de Santurce, we can easily buy ingredients directly from the source, and the plaza offers a fantastic look into daily life in San Juan. Visiting Santaella is to experience what I love—the collaborations

among friends, lively conversations filled with humor, the celebration of food and drink, and you may even walk in to find me singing in the dining room. My team and I are so happy to have a place for people to gather and experience our interpretation of Puerto Rico.

This book represents where I have been and what I want to show the world of *cocina tropical*. It's been a journey for me as I drift through my memories and recall those who have influenced me, and also an opportunity to take a deeper look into my heritage and the history of my home. My hope is you will taste the depth of flavors in my interpretation of the island's cuisine, and that you too will be drawn to the joy that can be experienced around the lively Puerto Rican table.

Opposite: Jose Santaella with his friend and mentor Alfredo Ayala.
Above: Santaella restaurant. *Right:* Jose Santaella.
Overleaf, clockwise from top left: A *kiosko* in Piñones; sea grapes; pineapple and citrus; Flamenco Beach on Culebra island; fresh green coconuts; overlooking the Cayo Luis Peña off Culebra island; whole red snapper fried over an open fire; the cobblestone steets in Old San Juan; a cook prepares yellow rice.

COSAS PARA PICAR

Hors d'Oeuvres

The aroma of savory snacks gurgling in oil is part of the ether in Puerto Rico. Throughout this book are many recipes for frituras, or fritters, made from some of the numerous and diverse root vegetables that are common on the island. They are delicious alone, with a little salt, or as a crunchy vehicle for delicious toppings like this homemade sausage. Making sausage from scratch may seem intimidating, but it is not as complicated as it sounds. Once you get the hang of filling the casings, you will want to start making sausage out of everything! This particular sausage is a mixture of pork, garlic, spices, and cilantro—a very *criollo* combination.

FRITURAS DE YUCA CON LONGANIZA DE CERDO
Cassava Fritters with Pork Sausage

MAKES ABOUT 24 FRITTERS

1 pound cassava (yuca) root (see page 27), peeled
  Vegetable oil, for deep-frying
3 Pork Longaniza Sausage Links (recipe on page 108)
1 tablespoon olive oil
  Kosher salt
  Cilantro leaves, for garnish

Cut the cassava root crosswise into 3-inch pieces. Cut those pieces lengthwise and remove the stringy and fibrous core. Grate the cassava on the side of a box grater with the smallest holes.

In a large, heavy saucepan, heat 3 inches of vegetable oil over high heat to 350°F. Line a plate with paper towels.

Carefully drop a tablespoon of the grated cassava into the hot oil and fry until golden brown, about 2 minutes. Transfer the fritter from the oil to a heatproof surface and, using the back of a metal spatula, flatten it into a round, 1-inch patty. Return to the oil for 1 minute, or until golden brown and crispy. Using a slotted spatula, transfer to the paper towel–lined plate to drain. Repeat the process with the remaining grated cassava.

Put the sausage links in a medium saucepan and add water to cover. Bring to a boil and cook for 2 to 3 minutes. Remove from the water and pat dry. Let cool to room temperature, then finely chop the sausage. In a skillet, sauté the sausage in the olive oil over medium-high heat for 1 minute or until heated through.

Spoon a small amount of the sausage onto each cassava fritter, garnish with the cilantro, and serve immediately as canapés.

NOTE: If you want to make the sausage from scratch, start five days in advance so it will have time to cure. You may be able to find ready-made Puerto Rican longaniza sausage in international markets; you can also substitute Spanish chorizo.

The starchy tubers of the Caribbean are arguably the most important staple in our food system's catalog. Yautia is the Taino Indian name for taro root. Brown and a bit hairy on the outside, the yautia is often mistaken for another tuber that we call malanga. They are quite similar and you may actually see them displayed in the same bin at your grocery store. No matter what the name, you can use either of these tubers in this recipe. Grated and tossed with just a little salt, small spoonfuls of yautia are fried, then coated in sugar. Even though the fritters are tossed in sugar, they are traditionally served as an appetizer. Their sweetness is a nice contrast to other salty snacks that might be served.

FRITURAS DE YAUTIA CON AZÚCAR

Yautia Fritters Tossed with Sugar

MAKES ABOUT 24 FRITTERS

2   pounds white yautia
     (see page 27)
1½ tablespoons kosher salt
     Vegetable oil, for deep-frying
1   cup granulated sugar

Wash and peel the yautia, then grate the tuber using the smallest holes on a standard box grater. In a large bowl, mix the grated yautia together with the salt.

In a heavy skillet, heat 3 inches of oil over high heat to 350°F. Using a tablespoon, carefully drop rounded spoonfuls of the yautia into the hot oil and fry until golden brown, about 4 minutes. Avoid overcrowding the pan. Using a slotted spoon, transfer the yautia from the oil and drain in a colander.

In a large bowl, toss the warm fried yautia in the sugar to coat. Serve immediately.

Puerto Rican cooks typically don't use a lot of gadgets.

Our cuisine is born out of the methods of the Taíno Indians, who inhabited the island originally, the Spanish who landed here with techniques and ingredients brought from the Old World, the Africans who were brought to the New World to work fields and cook, and the more modern influx of people from around the globe. The tools we use most often are simple but effective pieces that are so essential to our recipes that they are as important as the ingredients themselves. You can find these tools online or in international markets and, when you are in San Juan, head to the Plaza del Mercado de Santurce, where fresh fruits, vegetables, meat, and fish but also many household essentials are sold.

CALDERO Similar in size and shape to a Dutch oven, this cooking pot is deep and wide, with a tight-fitting lid; it's usually made from thick cast aluminum. The metal is a great conductor of heat and is strong but fairly light. Many cooks have a prized *caldero*, a pot that they always use for a certain recipe or for cooking rice. It might be dented and discolored, but it is precious and very often a vessel that has been passed down for generations.

GRATER In many recipes here, starchy root vegetables and green bananas and plantains must be grated to achieve the proper texture. Investing in a simple box grater is important if you want to make the cassava, yautia, and *malanga* fritters in this chapter or the green banana and root vegetable *alcapurrias* on page 36. A food processor will not yield the same texture, and it can often bruise the vegetable or fruit, changing its texture and quality.

MACHETE The machete is used for all kinds of tasks. Often men will carry a small, eight-inch-long machete in a belted sheath around their waist—a sort of Puerto Rican pocket knife. Walking through a field or in the lush mountains, the machete is easily drawn and used to hack through brushy paths. Street vendors wield them to lop off the tops of coconuts before sticking in straws and handing them to customers. In the *lechoneras* of Guavate, the cooks and pitmasters use large, very sharp machetes to chop through the crisp skin, meat, and bones of the cooked pigs.

PILÓN A *pilón* is a mortar and pestle. The act of smashing ingredients and grinding them between two stones is literally a Stone Age technique, and the *pilón* that we now use is not very far removed from what those first cooks used. From smooth polished marble, to grainier, textured stone, to the wooden ones that we use in Puerto Rico, the inside surface of the *pilón* affects the end result of whatever is being ground. We use a wooden *pilón* to prepare mofongo (see page 147).

TOSTONERA This simple tool is nothing more than two smooth wood-handled paddles hinged together, but the *tostonera* dramatically speeds up the process of making tostones—double-fried plantains. Sections of starchy plantains must be mashed flat before frying, and the wood paddles aid in applying even pressure to the chunks, resulting in tostones of consistent size and shape.

Roast chicken, perfect in its simplicity, is an anchor of a recipe that keeps a kitchen stable. Taking the time to roast chicken for this chicken salad recipe deepens the flavor at a base level. The malanga (or cocoyam) root is grated and fried into a crispy shingle, a mild, nutty-flavored base for this tarragon-scented roast chicken salad. The chicken salad can be made in advance and kept covered in the refrigerator overnight—and in fact this allows time for the flavors to blend together well.

FRITURAS DE MALANGA CON POLLO ASADO AL TARRAGÓN
Cocoyam Fritters with Roasted Chicken

MAKES 24 FRITTERS

1 (5- to 6-pound) roasting chicken, cleaned and rinsed

3 tablespoons olive oil
Kosher salt and freshly ground black pepper

½ head of garlic

½ orange
Vegetable oil, for deep-frying

1 pound cocoyam (see page 27), peeled and finely grated

2 cups mayonnaise (page 106)

1 cup honey mustard

1 tablespoon balsamic vinegar

3 tablespoons finely chopped shallots

¼ cup chopped fresh tarragon, plus whole leaves for garnish

Preheat the oven to 350°F.

Rub the outside and inside of the chicken with the olive oil, then season with salt and pepper. Place the garlic and the orange inside the chicken. Place the chicken in a roasting pan and roast for about 1½ hours, or until the juices run clear when the chicken is cut between a leg and thigh. Remove from the oven and set aside until cool enough to handle safely.

Remove the meat from the bones and very finely dice it. Place the meat in a large bowl and cool in the refrigerator for 2 hours. Discard the bones and skin or reserve them for another use.

Meanwhile, in a large, heavy saucepan, heat 3 inches of vegetable oil over high heat to 350°F. Line a plate with paper towels.

Carefully drop a tablespoon of the grated cocoyam into the hot oil and fry until golden brown, about 2 minutes. Transfer the fritter from the oil to a heatproof surface and using, the back of a metal spatula, flatten it into a round, 1-inch patty. Return to the hot oil for 1 minute, or until golden brown and crispy. Using a slotted spatula, transfer to the paper towel–lined plate to drain. Repeat the process with the remaining grated cocoyam.

In a medium bowl, stir together the mayonnaise, honey mustard, vinegar, shallots, ½ teaspoon salt, ½ teaspoon pepper, and the chopped tarragon. Add the mayonnaise mixture to the chopped chicken and stir until well combined. Cover and place in the refrigerator for 1 hour.

Spoon a small amount of the chicken mixture onto each cocoyam fritter. Garnish with the tarragon leaves and serve immediately.

ROOT VEGETABLES

The broad category of *viandas*, or root vegetables, is essential to our cuisine, not just because the earthy flavors pair so well with the deep layers of so many dishes here but also because they represent a traditional way for budget-constrained farming families especially to provide excellent nutrition and satisfying bulk to large numbers of people.

These vegetables are not simply regarded as humble, starchy fillers—they are a celebrated part of our culture. They are just as important to Puerto Rican cuisine as seafood and meat, and I like to think of them as exotic options for a healthful vegetarian diet. The importance of these *viandas*—the word's etymological profile is based on the Latin root for "meat"—cannot be overstated. Considered the base—almost the meat—of our cuisine, many of them were here long before Old World ships made their way across the ocean, and some of them, brought along on those ships hauling goods and people from Europe and Africa, are now thought of as native plants.

Clockwise from top left: eggplant (although not a root vegetable, this is a popular ingredient, and this purple variety is the one used most often in Puerto Rico); *ñame*; *apio; malanga; pana; batata; chayote*; yautia (center, cut in half); *calabaza*; cassava.

APIO Indigenous to Puerto Rico and an important part of the Taíno Indian diet, this starchy root vegetable is similar in appearance to celeriac (celery root), but quite different in taste. In contrast to the strong, almost pungent taste of celery root, *apio* is mild and has a texture similar to that of white potatoes. *Apio* can be cooked and used the same way as white potatoes.

BATATA *Batata* is the word we use to refer to sweet potatoes. *Batatas* come in a rainbow of colors ranging from white to yellow, rose, orange, red, and even purple. We typically use the paler varieties—white and yellow—as they are less sweet and have a slightly drier, starchier texture than the deeper-colored potatoes.

PANA Though the spiny pod-shaped breadfruit grows on a large tree, its flesh is quite starchy and when cooked has a taste and texture similar to potatoes. Thus it's often thought of as one of our *viandas*, even though it's not a root vegetable. The cooked fruit has also been described as having the yeasty taste and smell of fresh baked bread, hence its name *panapen* or *pana* for short. Breadfruit is an easygoing kitchen companion that takes well to boiling, baking, sautéing, or steaming; it pairs well as a side to any number of dishes. (By the way, in Puerto Rico, when you call someone a *pana*, it means he or she is a good friend.) The bright green, prickly underripe fruit provides the most starch; the yellowish green fruit with skin that is slightly smoother is used both as a savory and sweet base; and the slightly overripe breadfruit that is sweet and creamy can be used in desserts.

CALABAZA This tropical pumpkin, also known as West Indian pumpkin, is native to the island and was historically a very valuable part of the Taíno diet. Though not a tuber, it is prepared in much the same way as root vegetables. These large squash are of ancient origin and while their exteriors may vary a bit in color and texture, the ones found in Puerto Rico are a squat, round pumpkin with orange flesh and a mildly sweet flavor.

CASSAVA It's incredible that the pre-Columbian Indians figured out how to use this root, otherwise known as yuca, tapioca, and manioc. To be rendered edible, the flesh of the cassava root must be peeled and cooked. A staple crop to the Taíno Indians then, the cassava is still just as important: A vital part of world nutrition, it is the third most consumed starch after rice and corn.

MALANGA This root, also known as cocoyam, is often mistaken for taro root because it looks almost identical, with its irregular, oblong shape and brown, hairy exterior. The *malanga* has a mild, earthy-tasting yellow or cream-colored flesh that is moist and crunchy. It behaves well when simmered, used as a thickening agent in soups and stews, but it can be fried as well.

ÑAME A versatile root vegetable, *ñame* is an African yam. It is a gnarled, brown tuber that can grow to be a couple of feet long. Usually boiled like a potato, *ñame* can also be baked or ground to a flour. The taste is like that of *malanga* but very starchy with a somewhat grainy texture.

YAUTIA Also known as taro root, yautia grows naturally under the forest canopy but can also be easily cultivated in fields with direct sunlight. The tuber's ability to be grown in various conditions has secured its importance in many tropical food systems. Although it is cooked like a potato, it has a distinct nuttiness in flavor.

The Puerto Rican love of pork yields myriad recipes utilizing every part of the animal. We have a deep respect for the traditions associated with cooking a pig, and one of the most delicious recipes that comes from the process is morcilla, or blood sausage. Because the blood of the pig must be used very soon after it is slaughtered, many of the masters of *lechón*, or barbecue as you may know it, have also perfected the art of making this sausage. Morcilla is available all year round, but we especially like to eat it at Christmastime. This recipe is a nice way to incorporate morcilla into a party food that is easy to serve as a passed appetizer.

SPRING ROLLS DE MORCILLA CON MAYONESA DE PIQUE PUERTORRIQUEÑO
Blood Sausage Spring Rolls with Pique Mayo

MAKES 12 SPRING ROLLS

12   spring roll wrappers (thawed if frozen)
2   large eggs, lightly beaten
12   ounces fresh morcilla (blood sausage, see page 31), removed from the casing
     Vegetable oil, for deep-frying
     Spicy Mayo (recipe follows)

Place the spring roll wrappers on a work surface and brush lightly with the beaten egg. Spread 1 ounce of the morcilla in the middle of each wrapper. Fold one of the edges of the wrapper over the morcilla, fold in the sides of the wrapper, and roll up.

In a large, heavy pot, heat 3 inches of vegetable oil to 350°F. Fry the spring rolls for about 2 minutes, turning once or twice, until golden brown and crisp. Drain the rolls on paper towels and serve immediately with spicy mayo.

MAYONESA DE PIQUE PUERTORRIQUEÑO / PIQUE MAYO

MAKES 1 CUP

1   large egg yolk
1½   tablespoons fresh lemon juice
1   tablespoon white wine vinegar
1   small shallot, finely chopped
½   tablespoon Dijon mustard
      Kosher salt
¾   cup olive oil
2   tablespoons strained pique (page 40)
½   teaspoon freshly ground white pepper
2   tablespoons chopped cilantro

Whisk together the egg yolk, lemon juice, vinegar, shallot, mustard, and a pinch of salt until well combined. Add the oil a few drops at a time at first, then in a thin stream, whisking continuously until the mixture begins to thicken. Add the pique, white pepper, and cilantro, and whisk a few times to mix well. Taste and adjust the seasoning. Store in an airtight container in the refrigerator for up to 1 week.

MORCILLA

Dark and rich morcilla, a traditional blood sausage, is a beloved part of our culinary tradition.

Originating from a need and desire to utilize the entire animal when cooking a pig, the blood is the first thing harvested from the freshly slaughtered animal. Families who lived in the country would make a day of killing a hog, knowing that the work it took to slaughter and process the various parts for consuming, curing, and storing would need to be fast and efficient. The blood of the animal is taken and used immediately while it's perfectly fresh. With changing schedules and evolving work traditions, city dwellers and modern Puerto Ricans turn to butchers and *lechoneras* for their morcilla. Deep red and a little thick, the rich blood is mixed with rice, garlic, peppers, cilantro, and *culantro*—a bloody scene as the filling is piped into the casings. It's a bit unnerving to witness its production, but morcilla is a wonderful way to use an iron-rich ingredient that provides such amazing flavor. Once stuffed, the morcilla is then boiled and either sold fresh or frozen. When ready to eat, the sausage is cut into inch-long chunks and deep-fried or sautéed in a bit of oil in a hot skillet until the cut surfaces are seared and the meat is heated through. It can also be removed from the casing and mixed into recipes like the Blood Sausage Spring Rolls with Spicy Mayo on page 28. While morcilla is available year round, it is a traditional Christmas food, an irreplaceable part of our holiday celebrations.

My grandfather Alfonso Santaella, my father's father, was an elegant man—tall, thin, and always well-dressed. Affectionately known as "Abo," he worked hard all his life in the sugar industry that has thrived in Puerto Rico for centuries. After he retired, he moved close to where we lived in San Juan and we visited him quite often. He was a very good cook and had a few recipes that were his signature dishes. Every day he would make a soup of either chicken or beef with a clear broth. For an appetizer he would make these *almojábanas*—very simple and traditional fritters made from rice flour. Alfonso took a lot of pride in his cooking, and I'm lucky that I got to spend so much of my younger years with him. He died in 1990 at the age of ninety-nine, and I can't make these *almojábanas* without thinking of him.

ALMOJÁBANAS
Rice Flour Fritters

MAKES ABOUT 34 FRITTERS

- ½ cup whole milk
- ½ cup all-purpose flour
- 1 cup rice flour
- 1 tablespoon baking powder
- 1 teaspoon kosher salt
- 4 large eggs, separated
- 4 tablespoons (½ stick) butter, melted
- 1 cup grated or crumbled queso del país or other fresh white cheese (see Note)
- ½ cup freshly grated Parmesan cheese
  Vegetable oil, for deep-frying

In a large bowl, combine the milk, all-purpose flour, rice flour, baking powder, and salt. Add the egg yolks one at a time, whisking vigorously between each addition until well blended. Stir in the melted butter and both cheeses and set aside.

In the bowl of a stand mixer fitted with the whisk attachment, beat the egg whites on high speed until soft peaks form. Gently fold the egg whites into the egg yolk mixture.

In a heavy pot, heat 3 inches of oil over high heat to 350°F. Line a plate with paper towels.

Carefully drop rounded spoonfuls of the batter into the hot oil and fry until golden brown, about 2 minutes. Using a slotted spoon, transfer the fritters to the paper towel–lined plate to drain. Serve immediately.

NOTE: *Queso del país* is a fresh local cow's milk cheese that is easily crumbled. If you can't find Puerto Rican cheese, you can substitute ricotta salata or Mexican queso fresco.

One of the highlights of spending a day at the beach is the opportunity to eat from a *kiosko*, one of our famous roadside stands. The roads adjacent to Puerto Rico's popular beaches are lined with vendors selling traditional street food. Eating these codfish fritters with a Medalla beer is as much a part of a day at the beach as swimming and surfing. Each stand is equipped with pots of shimmering hot oil; a garlicky batter full of flaked salted codfish and flecks of cilantro is ladled in carefully to create a shallow, floating disk. The fritters are thin, allowing as much crisp surface area as possible, and once they have turned golden they are fished out with long skewers and hung to drain for a moment before being sold.

BACALAÍTOS
Codfish Fritters

MAKES 12 TO 15 FRITTERS

½ pound salt cod, de-salted (see Note)

2 cups all-purpose flour

1 teaspoon kosher salt

½ teaspoon freshly ground black pepper

½ teaspoon baking powder

2 cloves garlic, mashed to a paste in a mortar

2 tablespoons finely chopped fresh cilantro
Vegetable oil, for deep-frying

Fill a large bowl with ice water. Bring a pot of water to a boil and add the cod; boil for 2 minutes. Remove the fish with a slotted spoon and immediately immerse it in the ice water to stop the cooking. Once the fish is cool, pick the meat from the bones and flake the fish. Place the meat in a medium bowl. Add the flour, salt, pepper, baking powder, garlic, cilantro, and 2 cups water and mix well. Let stand at room temperature for 15 minutes.

In a deep, heavy skillet, heat 3 inches of the oil over medium-high heat to 350°F. Line a plate with paper towels.

Working in batches, ladle about ¼ cup of the batter at a time into the hot oil. The batter will spread out naturally and create a thin, flat fritter. Fry until golden brown on all sides, 4 to 5 minutes. Using a slotted spoon, transfer the fritters to the paper towel–lined plate to drain. Serve immediately.

NOTE: Because salt cod is preserved in layers of salt (another Spanish influence), you'll need to de-salt the fish before you cook it. Rinse the fish under cold running water, put it in a deep bowl, and cover with equal parts water and milk. (The milk causes the fish to become more flaky.) Soak it at room temperature overnight or in the refrigerator for up to 2 days. Drain well and proceed with the recipe.

Alcapurrias are standard fare at the *kioskos*, or roadside stands, near the beach. They are made from a mixture of grated green bananas, yautia, and either beef or land crab meat. The cooks in the kiosks are experts at taking a sea grape leaf (a plant that grows prolifically at the beach) in one hand, spreading the batter on the leaf, and then placing a dollop of filling into the center, wrapping the leaf around the batter to shape it, and carefully sliding the batter from the leaf into the hot oil (see page 51). The leaves are used just to shape the batter, not to be eaten. The beef filling for the *alcapurrias* can be made in advance, covered, and stored in the refrigerator for up to twenty-four hours or frozen for up to three months. Be sure to bring it back to room temperature before frying.

ALCAPURRIAS
Green Banana and Root Vegetable Fritters

MAKES 12 TO 14 FRITTERS

1   pound yautia (see page 27)
3   green bananas (see page 208)
1   tablespoon annatto oil (receipe on page 40), plus more for greasing
1   tablespoon kosher salt
½   pound ground beef
½   cup sofrito (recipe on page 40)
     Vegetable oil, for deep-frying
     Sea grape leaves, banana leaves cut into 3-by-4-inch pieces, or waxed paper sheets, for shaping the filling

Peel the yautia and green bananas. Rinse them under running water, then grate them on the large holes of a box grater. In a large bowl, combine the grated yautia and bananas, the annatto oil, and the salt and mix well. Set aside.

In a skillet, cook the ground beef with the sofrito over medium-high heat until the meat is fully browned, about 5 minutes. Set aside.

In a large, heavy saucepan, heat 3 inches of oil over high heat to 350°F. Line a plate with paper towels.

Hold a piece of waxed paper in one hand (or a banana or sea grape leaf if you have one), and grease lightly with some of the annatto oil. Spread about 3 tablespoons of the banana mixture onto the paper. Spoon 1 tablespoon of the ground beef filling in the center. Spoon enough banana mixture on top of the ground beef to cover, then shape into a 2-inch-long cylinder. Carefully slide the cylinder out of the paper and into the hot oil. Repeat to make a few more fritters, but don't crowd the oil. Fry until golden brown, 6 to 7 minutes. Using a slotted spoon, transfer the fritters to the paper towel–lined plate. Repeat with the remaining banana mixture and filling. Serve immediately.

SOFRITO

It's impossible to discuss Puerto Rican food without mentioning sofrito.

Our cuisine essentially begins with sofrito; it is the backbone of flavor in many of our dishes. Proper Puerto Rican sofrito is an aromatic sauté of garlic, tomatoes, onions, *culantro*, cilantro, and *ají dulce* and cubanelle peppers cooked in annatto oil flavored with bacon, salt pork, or cured ham. Bay leaf, cumin, *sazón* (a seasoned salt), and oregano can be added, along with *alcaparrado* (a mixture of pimento-stuffed olives and capers). The Spanish introduced the technique of building the flavors of a dish by starting with sofrito many centuries ago when they explored and settled in the Caribbean and what is now known as Latin America. At that point, the mixture may have been nothing more than oil and onions and possibly garlic. As people spread across the various lands that make up Latin America, sofrito morphed to take on the nuances of local ingredients and evolved according to the influence of indigenous people or the habits of the cooks in a certain place.

A sofrito in Cuba or the Dominican Republic will be very different from a Puerto Rican sofrito. To achieve a true Puerto Rican sofrito, it is very important to include cilantro, *alcaparrado*, and *culantro*, a broad-leaf aromatic herb (also called sawtooth cilantro, pictured at center of photo opposite, being chopped). *Culantro* has a flavor similar to that of cilantro but is much stronger—we use the two together in many recipes because the subtle differences in flavor complement each other. If you have a hard time finding *culantro*, you can simply use cilantro in its place. We sauté the mixture in bright yellow annatto-infused oil. Sofrito can be stored in the refrigerator for about a week or frozen for up to three months (some cooks freeze it in ice cube trays so it's easy to pull out a small bit at a time when needed). It is a common practice for home cooks and professionals alike to keep sofrito on hand at all times so that it is always available to start a recipe.

Sofrito serves as the foundation of almost every main dish in Puerto Rico—including a large number of those in this book. Other countries have their own versions, and even in households throughout our island each cook will put his or her own twist on it. The basic ingredients of a Puerto Rican sofrito, however, are always the same: onions, garlic, tomato paste, *ají dulce* peppers, cilantro, and *culantro*. Other flavorings will weave their way in and out, as in my version below, but the particulars listed above remain constant and are what make this staple undeniably Puerto Rican.

SOFRITO
Puerto Rican Flavor Base

MAKES 2 CUPS

- ½ cup olive oil
- 2 yellow onions, finely diced
- 10 cloves garlic, mashed to a paste in a mortar (see Notes)
- 1 tablespoon tomato paste
- ¼ cup diced smoked ham
- 1 ripe (but not too soft) tomato, diced
- 2 bay leaves
- ¼ cup seeded and chopped ají dulce peppers (see Notes) or other small sweet peppers
- 1 large cubanelle pepper (see Notes), finely diced
- 1 tablespoon dried oregano
- 1 tablespoon annatto oil (recipe follows)
- 3 tablespoons alcaparrado (see Notes)
- 1 tablespoon kosher salt, or more to taste
- 4 fresh culantro leaves
- 3 tablespoons chopped fresh cilantro

In a large skillet, heat the oil over medium-high heat. Add the onions and sauté, stirring, for about 2 minutes. Stir in the garlic and tomato paste and cook for 1 minute. Add the ham and cook, stirring, for about 1 minute. Stir in the tomato, bay leaves, ají dulce and cubanelle peppers, oregano, annatto oil, alcaparrado, and salt and cook until the onions become translucent. Remove from the heat and add the culantro and cilantro. Taste and adjust the seasoning. Let cool and use immediately or store, sealed, in the refrigerator for up to 3 days or in the freezer for up to 1 month.

ANNATTO OIL

Annatto or achiote oil is made from the colorful seeds of the achiote tree. The seeds are used in many parts of the world to impart a natural yellow, orange, or red color to many foods (the color depends on the amount of annatto used). In Puerto Rico, we often use oil that has been infused with annatto seeds—primarily for the vibrant color it imparts to dishes, but also for the mild earthy and faintly peppery flavor it adds. Annatto oil looks quite similar to the red palm oil that is essential to West African cooking.

MAKES 1 CUP

- ¼ cup annatto (achiote) seeds
- 1 cup vegetable or olive oil

In a small saucepan combine the annatto seeds and the oil and place over low heat. Bring the oil to a simmer, stirring the seeds around occasionally, for about 10 minutes. Remove from the heat and allow the oil to cool for about 15 minutes before straining the oil through a sieve into a clean bowl or jar, discarding the seeds. Once cool, the oil can be sealed and refrigerated for up to 3 months.

NOTES: In practically every recipe that calls for garlic in Puerto Rico, the garlic is mashed to a pulp in a mortar and pestle, an essential tool in the Puerto Rican kitchen that's also used for grinding and smashing herbs. You can also just mash the peeled garlic against a cutting board several times with the side of a knife until it becomes a paste.

Ají dulce peppers are little lantern-shaped peppers that look like habañeros but are sweet rather than hot. You may substitute any small, sweet red pepper. Cubanelle peppers are medium-size green peppers; you could substitute a green bell pepper.

Alcaparrado is a simple mixture of green olives, capers, pimento, vinegar, and oil. You can find it in jars in good grocery stores and online.

A BEACHSIDE BARBECUE

—

MENU

—

EMPANADILLAS DE PULPO
Octopus Turnovers, page 44

DIP DE CEBOLLA CON BATATA FRITA
Caramelized Onion Dip with Sweet Potato Chips, page 69

LANGOSTA A LA BARBACOA CON MANTEQUILLA DE SOFRITO
Grilled Rock Lobster, page 175

ENSALADA DE PAPA
Potato Salad with Olives and Pimentos, page 176

ENSALADA DE AGUACATE, PAPAYA, CHINA Y TORONJA
Avocado and Papaya Salad, page 179

BRAZO GITANO DE PARCHA
Passion Fruit Roulade, page 222

BEER

There are certain roads on the island that hold very specific memories and strong associations for me. Some lead to the rainforest, others to Piñones, and another to Guavate, where the famous barbecue *lechoneras* are located. Each destination has a flavor attached to it, and just the act of getting in the car and turning onto one of these roads elicits a specific craving in me. There is a lovely area on the opposite side of the island from San Juan called Ponce. We would go there fairly often when I was a child. Roadside food stands are common all over the island, but the ones in Ponce offer *empanadillas* (little turnovers); my favorites are the *empanadillas de pulpo*—octopus turnovers.

EMPANADILLAS DE PULPO
Octopus Turnovers

MAKES 24 EMPANADILLAS

FOR THE FILLING:

- 3 pounds octopus meat (or a whole octopus), thawed if frozen (see Note)
- 1 yellow onion, quartered, plus 1 yellow onion, chopped
- 1 bay leaf
- 1 tablespoon smoked paprika
- 3 tablespoons olive oil
- 3 cloves garlic, mashed to a paste in a mortar
- 1 tablespoon tomato paste
- 2 tablespoons tomato sauce
- 3 tablespoons chopped fresh cilantro
- ½ cup roughly chopped green olives
- 1 carrot, finely diced
  Kosher salt and freshly ground black pepper

FOR THE DOUGH:

- 4 cups all-purpose flour, plus more for dusting
- 2 teaspoons kosher salt
- 1¾ cups shortening
- 1 large egg, lightly beaten
- ½ cup ice water
  Vegetable oil, for deep-frying

MAKE THE FILLING: Place the octopus, quartered onion, bay leaf, and ½ tablespoon of the smoked paprika in a large stockpot. Cover with water by at least 2 inches. Bring to a boil over high heat, then reduce the heat to medium and cook until the octopus is tender, 45 minutes to 1 hour. Remove from the heat and allow to cool in the pot for about an hour. Drain the octopus and discard the onion and bay leaf. Cut out the hard beak and discard. Place the head and tentacles on a cutting board and slice the octopus into ¼-inch pieces.

Heat the oil in a large saucepan over medium-high heat. Add the chopped onion and sauté until the onion is translucent, about 4 minutes. Add the garlic, tomato paste, and tomato sauce and cook, stirring continuously, for about 3 minutes. Remove from the heat and add the cilantro, olives, the remaining ½ tablespoon smoked paprika, the carrot, and the octopus and mix well. Add salt and pepper to taste and set aside.

MAKE THE DOUGH: In a large bowl, combine the flour, salt, and shortening using your hands or a pastry blender until pea-size crumbles form. Add the egg and water and mix until just combined and the dough forms a ball. Divide the dough into 15 equal portions. On a lightly floured surface, roll out one piece of the dough into a 6-inch circle. Place ⅓ cup of the filling on one half of the dough circle, leaving a ¾-inch border around the filling. Lightly brush the edge of the circle with some water and fold the dough over the filling to make a half-moon. Press out any excess air, pinch to seal, and press the edges with a fork to make a decorative edge and seal it completely. Repeat with the remaining dough portions and filling.

In a heavy saucepan, heat 2 inches of vegetable oil over medium-high heat to 350°F. Line a plate with paper towels.

Gently place the turnovers in the hot oil and fry, turning once or twice, until golden brown, about 5 minutes. Remove from the oil and transfer to the paper towel–lined plate to drain. Serve hot.

NOTE: Octopus is common in Puerto Rico, but finding fresh octopus elsewhere can be a challenge as it's highly perishable. Frozen octopus is much more widely available and is a fine substitute.

Rabbits raised on farms make a lovely product for the table. The meat is akin to that of the dark meat of a chicken or turkey. Rabbit legs are easy to sauté into a fricassee, and the resulting sauce that is created with sofrito, tomatoes, and a bit of orange zest is a bright accompaniment. This rabbit fricassee would also be nice as a main course served with rice, but shredding the meat, mixing in a bit of the sauce, and spooning it on top of these crunchy breadfruit tostones makes an elegant and unexpected canapé. The breadfruit is cut into chunks, then fried, smashed flat, and fried again. You can do the first frying and smashing up to 3 hours in advance; lay the pieces out in a single layer, cover, and refrigerate until ready to fry the second time, just before serving.

TOSTONES DE PANA CON FRICASE DE CONEJO
Double-Fried Breadfruit with Rabbit Stew

SERVES 12

1 medium breadfruit (see page 27), peeled
  Vegetable oil, for deep-frying
6 fresh rabbit legs
1 cup heavy cream
1 cup dry white wine
½ cup annatto oil (page 40)
  Finely grated zest of 1 orange
2 tablespoons dried oregano
6 cloves garlic, mashed to a paste in a mortar
¼ cup olive oil
2 cups sofrito (page 40)
  Kosher salt
1 tablespoon tomato paste
3 cups chicken stock
2 carrots, peeled and cut into small pieces

Cut the breadfruit in half lengthwise and remove and discard the soft core. Cut the fruit into 1-inch pieces.

In a large, heavy saucepan, heat 3 inches of vegetable oil over medium-high heat to 350°F. Line a plate with paper towels.

Carefully place the pieces of breadfruit in the hot oil and fry for about 5 minutes. Transfer from the oil to a heatproof surface and crush with the bottom of a skillet into a 1-inch round. Return to the oil and fry for 5 minutes more or until golden. Using a slotted spoon, transfer to the paper towel–lined plate to drain.

In a large bowl, combine the rabbit legs, cream, wine, annatto oil, orange zest, oregano, and garlic and let marinate at room temperature for 2 hours or in the refrigerator for up to 6 hours. In a large skillet (caldero), combine the olive oil and sofrito and cook over medium-high heat for about 2 minutes. Add the tomato paste and cook for 1 minute. Add the rabbit legs and their marinade to the skillet and stir to combine. Add the stock and carrots, reduce the heat to medium, and stir to combine. Cover and cook for 1 hour, stirring occasionally. Uncover and continue to cook for 15 minutes more, reducing the sauce slightly. Remove from the heat.

Remove the rabbit legs from the sauce, allow to cool just a bit, then pull the meat from the bones. Pull the meat apart using your hands to make bite-size pieces. Put the meat in a bowl with a few spoonfuls of the sauce and mix together. If the mixture seems too dry, add a bit more sauce.

Top each breadfruit tostone with a bit of the rabbit stew. Serve warm as a canapé.

This recipe is inspired by a traditional local dish that we call *arroz a caballo,* meaning "horseback rice." Simply white rice with a fried egg on top, this snack is sometimes also topped with sautéed baby bananas or *guineitos niños,* which are much sweeter than regular bananas. Once I started traveling the world, I realized that many other cultures have very similar variations on the same dish. Rice mixed with local ingredients and topped with a fried egg is a constant worldwide. It's fantastic when you experience these common dishes firsthand and it becomes very clear that different cultures are alike in many ways. Here, I have transformed this humble dish into an hors d'oeuvres elegant enough to be passed at a cocktail party.

CANAPÉ DE ARROZ A CABALLO
Rice Fritters with Baby Bananas and Quail Eggs

SERVES 8

- 2 teaspoons kosher salt, plus more as needed
- 2 cups short- or medium-grain white rice
  Vegetable oil, for deep-frying
- 3 to 4 baby bananas
- 1 tablespoon butter
- 8 quail eggs
- 1 tablespoon olive oil
  Freshly ground black pepper
- 8 fresh oregano or cilantro leaves, for garnish
  Pique or spicy mayo (page 61 or 28; optional)

In a medium saucepan, combine 4½ cups water and the salt and bring to a boil over high heat. Stir in the rice and return the water to a boil. Reduce the heat to medium-low, cover, and cook for 10 minutes. Stir again and cook the rice for 5 minutes more, until it looks sticky. There should be virtually no liquid left in the pan. Remove from the heat and let cool until it's safe to handle. You can speed up the cooling process by spreading the rice out on a baking sheet.

In a saucepan, heat 3 to 4 inches of vegetable oil over medium-high heat to 350°F. Line a plate with paper towels.

Take a small handful of rice and form it into a small patty. Repeat to make a total of 8 patties. Carefully slide the patties into the hot oil and fry each rice cake for about 1 minute on each side until golden and crisp. Using a spatula, transfer to the paper towel–lined plate to drain.

Peel and slice the bananas into ¼-inch-thick disks. In a skillet, melt the butter over medium heat. Add the bananas and sauté until they start to caramelize, about 2 minutes. Remove skillet from heat.

In another skillet, heat the olive oil over medium heat. Gently crack the quail eggs using the edge of a knife and carefully slide the eggs into the skillet. Fry sunny side up for about 1 minute, until the egg whites are firm but the yolk is still a little runny.

Place 3 or 4 slices of banana on top of each rice cake. Place 1 fried quail egg on top of the bananas and sprinkle with salt and pepper. Garnish with the oregano leaves and pique, if desired, and serve immediately.

Just a few miles outside of San Juan, traveling east on Route 187, the metropolitan feel of the city fades away and you enter the area known as Piñones, home to a wonderful beach and Bosque Estatal de Piñones, a forest reserve where generations of Puerto Ricans have gone to escape the city on weekends and on days off work. To the left of the road is the beach—miles of gorgeous, wide sandy swaths filled with sunbathers, families, and surfers—without any tall buildings nearby. To the right, rustic, independently owned kiosks are lined up, each with its own identity, hoping to lure you in to taste the food.

Clockwise from top left: Lines often form outside each *kiosko*; a rooster polices his domain; a *bacalaito* fritter is skewered to cool and let excess oil drain away; cooks at a *kiosko* in Piñones; a cook spreads the batter for an *alcapurria* on a sea grape leaf before filling; conch salad squeezed with lime; open-air seating at a *kiosko*.

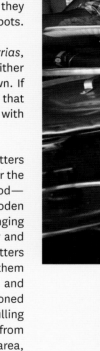

The kiosk vendors are islanders who claim African descent. The food they cook tends toward the traditional cuisines of West Africa—including dried, salted fish (*bacalao*), and rice. There is a lot of competition among the vendors, so to attract customers they decorate their spaces with brightly colored hand-painted signs and flags. They play great salsa and merengue music in their bid to get your business. Some people have their favorites that they visit every time they go to the beach, while some of us like to try different spots.

The standard fare is deep-fried treats like *alcapurrias*, cod fritters, and tostones, chicken kebabs, and either fresh coconut water or a cold beer to wash it all down. If you order coconut water, there's a very good chance that someone will pull out a whole coconut, cut off the top with a machete, stick a straw in it, and hand it to you.

The cooks are in plain sight, just inside the open shutters of the kiosk. A man is constantly stoking the fires under the gurgling, oil-filled caldrons, using all manner of wood—some chopped tree wood, but mostly broken-down wooden shipping pallets—a great way to recycle! One cook, singing along to the lively music, will drop ladlefuls of batter and cod meat into the shimmering oil, and flat, lacy fritters form. The cook removes the fritters and skewers them over a warm part of the fire to allow them to drain and keep them warm. Another cook skillfully spoons seasoned mashed green banana or plantain wrapped around a filling of either meat, chicken, or land crab, cradling a leaf from the sea grape plant, which grows all over the beach area, in her hand to shape the dumpling into a plump oblong bundle. She then carefully slides the bundle into the hot oil until it turns a burnished brown.

The entire experience is nostalgic for natives and exciting for tourists. The communal open-air seating around wooden tables covered in brightly colored oilcloth is part of the charm. The ocean calls from one side and the forest of mangrove trees beckons you from the other. A visit to the kiosks at Piñones is a beautiful view into one aspect of Puerto Rican life and culture.

Growing up in San Juan is incredible. The city, while home to our island's government and diverse businesses, is also vibrant with music and color. The beach is within earshot, and when I was a kid I could walk home from school with my friends and go straight to the beach or a park. Almost every day after school, I would duck into one of the Spanish *panaderías*, or sandwich shops, that are all over the city. I had a standard order—a ham croquette. These very common Spanish-style snacks are not refined at all. They are simple—and, honestly, sometimes a little dry—but they were always satisfying and hold a place in my heart. Once I learned to cook I discovered that stirring in a béchamel created a velvety texture and I fell in love with *croquetas de jamón* all over again.

CROQUETAS DE JAMÓN Y CILANTRO
Ham and Cilantro Béchamel Croquettes

MAKES 6 CROQUETTES

- 1 cup milk
- 2½ tablespoons butter
- 2½ tablespoons all-purpose flour
- 1 teaspoon kosher salt, plus more as needed
- 1 teaspoon garlic powder
- 4 ounces good-quality cured ham, finely chopped
- 2 tablespoons chopped fresh cilantro
- ½ teaspoon freshly grated nutmeg
- 2 large eggs, lightly beaten
- 1 cup panko bread crumbs
- 1 cup potato flakes
- 1 cup finely ground Ritz or saltine cracker crumbs
- Peanut or vegetable oil, for deep-frying

In a small saucepan over medium-high heat, bring the milk to a boil, then remove from the heat and set aside. In another saucepan over low heat, melt the butter completely. Add the flour, salt, and garlic powder and cook, whisking, until the mixture is well blended. Gradually add the hot milk, whisking continuously until the mixture is completely blended and smooth. Increase the heat to medium-high and bring to a boil, whisking; cook for another 1 minute, then remove from the heat. Pour the béchamel into a bowl, let cool to room temperature, then add the ham, cilantro, and nutmeg. Fold the mixture into a paste. Cover the béchamel completely with plastic wrap, pressing down so that the plastic is touching the surface of the mixture to prevent a skin from forming. Refrigerate overnight.

The next day, heat at least 3 inches of oil in a heavy pot over medium-high heat to 350°F. Line a plate with paper towels.

While the oil is heating, beat the eggs in a small bowl and set aside. In a separate bowl, mix together the panko, potato flakes, and cracker crumbs.

Remove the chilled béchamel mixture from the refrigerator and, using a spoon or a small ice cream scoop or even your hands, scoop out portions of the paste and form them into approximately 1½-inch round croquettes. Set the croquettes on a baking sheet lined with parchment or waxed paper. Dip each croquette in the beaten egg and then roll in the bread crumbs mixture. In batches, carefully place the croquettes in the hot oil and fry until golden brown about 2 minutes. Using a slotted spoon, transfer the croquettes to the paper towel–lined plate to drain. Serve immediately, or keep warm in a 200°F oven until ready to serve.

NOTE: For this recipe you can use any good cured ham. It can be country ham, Serrano, or prosciutto, finely chopped with a knife or pulsed in a food processor.

Chopped chicken liver is one of those delicious recipes that is a bit of a throwback to the days of elegant cocktail hours and dinner parties with passed hors d'oeuvres. Pâté and terrine are back in fashion, and this dish falls right into step with them. The richness of the velvety liver and the sweetness of the caramelized onions get a tangy, tropical hit from the mango with a bit of peppery bite from the watercress garnish. Serve as-is for a small-plate appetizer, or spread the liver on smaller crostini for a perfect party bite.

TOSTADAS DE HÍGADO DE POLLO CON CEBOLLAS CARAMELIZADAS, MANGÓ, Y BERROS

Chicken Liver Toasts with Caramelized Onions, Mango, and Watercress

---

SERVES 6

3	cups fresh chicken livers
1	cup heavy cream
½	cup light rum or brandy
2	tablespoons annatto oil (page 40)
½	tablespoon dried oregano
1	clove garlic, mashed to a paste in a mortar
2	tablespoons butter
1	large yellow onion, finely diced
6	slices crusty bread
3	tablespoons olive oil
	Kosher salt and freshly ground black pepper
1	ripe mango, peeled and diced
1	bunch watercress

In a large bowl, combine the livers, cream, rum, annatto oil, oregano, and garlic. Cover and refrigerate for 2 hours to marinate.

Meanwhile, heat the butter and onion in a saucepan over low heat and sauté until caramelized, about 45 minutes. Remove from the heat and set aside. Toast the bread slices until golden brown and set aside.

Drain the chicken livers, reserving the marinade. In a large saucepan, heat the olive oil over medium-high heat. Add the chicken livers and sauté until cooked through, 8 to 10 minutes. In a separate saucepan, bring the reserved marinade to a boil over medium-high heat, then reduce the heat to maintain a simmer and cook until the liquid has thickened, about 2 minutes. Remove from the heat and let cool. Roughly chop the livers. Put the cream mixture in a blender and blend until creamy. Taste and adjust the seasoning with salt and pepper. Fold the cream mixture into the chopped livers.

Place some of the chopped liver mixture on each piece of toast and top with a spoonful of the caramelized onions. Place a few pieces of the mango on top of the caramelized onions and garnish with some watercress leaves. Serve immediately.

A delicious ingredient that found its way to the Caribbean from Africa, okra is a common vegetable in Puerto Rico. While some people are put off by the viscous juice inside the pods, that "slime," as some put it, functions as an important thickener in stews. We also love okra fried—a cooking method that eliminates the slimy quality. Inspired by the traditional recipe for Italian squash blossoms that are fried with anchovies and cream inside, this fried okra works beautifully with a smooth anchovy sauce, an elegant way to serve something that is considered by many to be a distinctly humble vegetable.

QUIMBOMBÓ REBOZADO SERVIDO CON CREMA DE ANCHOAS
Fried Okra with Anchovy Cream Sauce

SERVES 8

FOR THE ANCHOVY CREAM SAUCE:

16 anchovy fillets
½ cup cream cheese, softened
3 tablespoons mayonnaise (page 106)
1 tablespoon chopped fresh parsley
1 teaspoon fresh lime juice
1 teaspoon kosher salt, or more to taste
½ teaspoon freshly ground black pepper, or more to taste

FOR THE FRIED OKRA:

    Vegetable oil, for deep-frying
1¼ cups all-purpose flour
1 teaspoon kosher salt
½ teaspoon freshly ground black pepper
1½ cups light beer
1 large egg, lightly beaten
8 fresh okra pods, halved lengthwise

MAKE THE ANCHOVY CREAM SAUCE: In a food processor, combine all of the ingredients and process until smooth. Transfer to a bowl, cover, and refrigerate for up to 24 hours. When ready to serve, stir the mixture, taste, and adjust the seasoning with salt and pepper. If the dip is too thick, stir in 1 to 2 tablespoons water.

MAKE THE FRIED OKRA: In a large, deep saucepan, heat at least 3 inches of oil over medium-high heat to 350°F. Line a plate with paper towels.

In a medium bowl, whisk together the flour, salt, pepper, beer, and egg until combined—some lumps may remain. Dip the okra halves into the batter and carefully drop them into the hot oil. Fry until golden brown, about 2 minutes. Using a slotted spoon, transfer to the paper towel–lined plate to drain. Serve immediately with the sauce.

Children playing on the shores of Puerto Rico love to chase the land-dwelling crabs that scurry along the sand and into the holes they dig for housing. These crabs have been a staple protein on the island for centuries. Once the crabs are caught, they need to be kept in a cage for a few days and fed with corn, fruits, and root vegetables to purge them and sweeten their meat. They are similar to the blue crabs that live underwater, so you can substitute regular crabmeat.

TOSTONES DE PLÁTANO VERDE CON SALMOREJO DE JUEYES
Double-Fried Green Plantains with Land Crab

MAKES 12 TOSTONES

5   tablespoons olive oil
2   tablespoons annatto oil (page 40)
1   yellow onion, finely diced
4   ají dulce peppers (see page 41), finely diced
1   cubanelle pepper, finely diced
1   tablespoon tomato paste
6   cloves garlic, mashed to a paste in a mortar
1½ pounds cooked crabmeat, picked over and any stray shell removed
1   teaspoon kosher salt
3   tablespoons chopped fresh cilantro
12 tostones (page 166)

In a large skillet, heat the olive oil and achiote oil over high heat. Add the onion and ají dulce and cubanelle peppers and sauté for 3 to 4 minutes. Add the tomato paste and the garlic and sauté for 1 to 2 minutes, then add the crabmeat and cook for 1 to 2 minutes more. Add the salt and cilantro and stir to combine.

Remove from the heat and place a spoonful of the crab mixture on top of each toston. Serve immediately.

Thinner and more of a vinegar hot sauce than some of the typical thicker sauces found in America, pique can be sprinkled on pretty much anything. We keep it on our tables to be shaken on top of any savory dishes where a bit of heat and brightness is desired.

PIQUE
Puerto Rican Hot Sauce

MAKES 1 QUART

4 to 6 ounces fresh pineapple peel (from about ½ pineapple)
½ cup white vinegar
½ cup apple cider vinegar
12 small hot chiles (see Note), halved lengthwise
2 cloves garlic, peeled
10 whole black peppercorns
1 fresh oregano sprig
1 fresh culantro leaf
¼ teaspoon kosher salt
2 to 3 tablespoons extra-virgin olive oil

In a saucepan, combine 2 cups water and the pineapple peel and bring to a boil. Remove from the heat and allow to infuse for 5 minutes. Pour through a strainer set over a bowl and discard the pineapple peel.

Sterilize a clean quart-size glass bottle or jar with a tight-fitting lid by submerging it in boiling water for 10 minutes. Drain and let air-dry.

Put the vinegars, chiles, garlic, peppercorns, oregano, culantro, and salt in the bottle. Pour in the pineapple water. Add the oil slowly, little by little, so it completely covers the surface (this will help to keep the vinegar mixture sealed so that mold cannot grow). Screw the cap on the bottle or stop it up with a cork, then set it aside for 1 week at room temperature. Then store in the refrigerator for up to 2 months.

NOTE: The chiles we use in Puerto Rico are called *ajíes picantes*. You can substitute any small hot pepper like a Thai chile pepper. Use a mixture of green and red, if you like.

PIQUE CRIOLLO

Pique is a condiment that is used in every kitchen and set at every table in Puerto Rico.

It's not uncommon to see bottles of pique hanging in bundles by ropes suspended from the rafters in kiosks and market booths looking like sparkling, brightly colored bouquets. Tourists love to buy the bottles, knowing that it will preserve a taste of Puerto Rico when they get back home. The sauce is more vinegary than spicy, and personal preference dictates how hot each batch will turn out. Caballero and habañero peppers might be used for heat, along with a custom mix of oregano, garlic, onions, peppercorns, cilantro, *culantro,* and cumin. The addition of either pineapple pieces or pineapple skin adds sweetness in tandem with more acid, plus a bit of tannic quality from the skin. Some recipes call for rum. Traditionally, most home cooks have made their own pique— it's easy to make, and it's not unusual to see all kinds of bottles being recycled as containers for homemade pique. Old soda, rum, and store-bought condiment bottles can be used as long as they have a tight-fitting lid and a mouth large enough to fit the whole peppers through.

We use pique the way many Southerners might sprinkle pepper vinegar on collard greens or over fried foods. The slightly spicy, vinegary jolt is a nice foil to the heaviness of fried foods. Pique can be used in recipes, like the Jibarito Mule cocktail on page 245, but mainly it serves as a condiment.

Both of my parents were wonderful cooks, and while they enjoyed fancy, refined foods, they also appreciated the simplicity of traditional Puerto Rican standards. These oblong cornsticks are popular in restaurants and at roadside kiosks, and are often made at home. My mother used to make these all the time when I was a little kid, filling them with Cheddar cheese or even American cheese that melted onto my chin when I would take a bite. My mom knew what kids liked, and while I love the homey quality of the ones that my mother made back then, I now prefer to use the traditional Edam cheese.

SORULLITOS DE MAÍZ RELLENOS DE QUESO DE BOLA
Cornmeal and Cheese Fritters

MAKES 18 TO 20 FRITTERS

1   teaspoon kosher salt
1½   cups finely ground yellow cornmeal
½   teaspoon granulated sugar
1¼   cups shredded Edam cheese
     Corn oil, for deep-frying
     Mayoketchup (recipe follows)

In a medium saucepan, bring 2 cups water and the salt to a boil. Add the cornmeal, reduce the heat to low, and cook, stirring continuously, for 4 to 5 minutes, until thickened. Remove from the heat. Stir in the sugar and let the mixture cool.

With your hands, shape 2 tablespoons of the dough into a canoe, fill with about 1 tablespoon of the cheese, and close the canoe shape to make a stick about 3 inches long. Repeat with the remaining dough.

In a deep, heavy skillet, heat 3 inches of oil over medium-high heat to about 350°F. Line a plate with paper towels.

Carefully place the sorullitos in the hot oil and fry until golden brown all over, 3 to 4 minutes. Using a slotted spoon, transfer to the paper towel–lined plate to drain. Serve hot with the mayoketchup alongside.

MAYOKETCHUP / MAYOKETCHUP

Mayoketchup is a condiment second only in popularity to pique in Puerto Rico. Despite its popularity, it has been in Puerto Rico only since the 1970s. Different variations on this simple sauce are served all over South America (and it's similar to sauces served with French fries in the western United States and in Europe).

MAKES 1½ CUPS

1   cup mayonnaise (page 106)
½   cup ketchup
1   clove garlic, mashed to a paste in a mortar
     Kosher salt to taste

In a bowl, mix all the ingredients until smooth. Store covered in the refrigerator for up to 2 weeks.

Many cultures have their own versions of deviled eggs, and I love how simply stirring in a signature ingredient can take a recipe around the globe. Cilantro is an important flavor in Puerto Rican cooking, and the addition of curry powder nods to the exotic spices that made their way to the Caribbean via the spice route. A garnish of bacon adds a bit of the all-important flavor of smoked pork that we love so much on our island.

HUEVOS ENDIABLADOS AL CILANTRO
Deviled Eggs with Cilantro

MAKES 20 HALVES

10 large eggs
1   teaspoon white vinegar
¼   cup cream cheese, softened
1   teaspoon kosher salt, or more to taste
¼   teaspoon freshly ground black pepper, or more to taste
1½ teaspoons curry powder
¾   cup mayonnaise (page 106)
1   teaspoon chopped fresh cilantro
½   teaspoon apple cider vinegar
5   slices bacon, cooked crisp, for serving

Gently place the eggs in a large saucepan and add cold water to cover by at least 1 inch. Add the white vinegar and a pinch of salt to the water. Bring to a boil over medium-high heat, then remove from the heat, cover the pot, and allow to sit for 12 to 15 minutes. Drain the hot water from the pot and pour cold water over the eggs. Let the eggs sit in the cold water for a few minutes to cool completely, then peel them.

Using a sharp knife, slice each egg in half lengthwise. Gently remove the yolks, being careful to keep the whites in perfect form. Place the yolks in a food processor along with the cream cheese, salt, pepper, and curry powder. Process until smooth. Transfer the yolk mixture to a bowl and gently stir in the mayonnaise until well incorporated. Taste and adjust the seasoning with salt and pepper. Cover the whites and the yolk mixture and refrigerate for at least 1 hour.

Meanwhile, in a small bowl, combine the cilantro and cider vinegar.

Remove the chilled yolk mixture from the refrigerator and spoon into a pastry bag fitted with either a large round or star-shaped tip (or simply left open without a tip inserted). Pipe the yolk mixture into the reserved egg white halves. Sprinkle the tops with the cilantro-vinegar mixture and garnish each with a small piece of bacon. Serve immediately.

One of my favorite snack foods as a child was potato chips with onion dip. I still love the combination, and when I got a little older it became one of the standard appetizers I'd serve when I would host "disco" parties at my house. (Nydia Caro records were in heavy rotation, and I was singing along to all of them.) I was a teenager then, and I suppose that's when I developed my flair for catering. I don't have as many disco parties these days, but I still like chips and dip (and still adore Nydia). Since I'm a professional chef now, I decided to develop a more sophisticated version, made with good ingredients. Sweet potatoes are a common ingredient in Puerto Rico (one heirloom sweet potato variety in the States is even named the Puerto Rico), and the barely sweet chips provide a nice contrast to the salty onion dip. Perfect as a weekend snack for your kids, as an offering at a disco party, or any time!

DIP DE CEBOLLA CON BATATA FRITA
Caramelized Onion Dip with Sweet Potato Chips

MAKES ABOUT 2½ CUPS DIP; SERVES 12 TO 15

FOR THE DIP:

- 2 tablespoons olive oil
- 2 yellow onions, diced
- ½ cup (4 ounces) cream cheese, at room temperature
- 1½ cups sour cream
- ¾ cup mayonnaise (page 106)
- ½ teaspoon balsamic vinegar
- ½ clove garlic, mashed to a paste in a mortar
- 1 tablespoon finely chopped fresh chives
- 2 tablespoons finely chopped scallions
- 1 teaspoon salt
- ½ teaspoon freshly ground white pepper

FOR THE CHIPS:

- 2 large sweet potatoes, peeled and sliced ⅛ inch thick
- 1 tablespoon salt, plus more for sprinkling
  Vegetable oil, for deep-frying

MAKE THE DIP: In a saucepan, heat the oil and onions over low heat. Sauté slowly, stirring occasionally, until the onions are caramelized, about 45 minutes. Remove from the heat and let cool for about 10 minutes.

In a large bowl, combine the cream cheese, sour cream, mayonnaise, vinegar, garlic, chives, scallions, salt, and white pepper and mix well. Stir in the caramelized onions. Taste and adjust the seasoning with salt and white pepper. Cover and refrigerate until ready to serve, up to 2 days.

MAKE THE CHIPS: Put the sweet potato slices in a bowl and cover with cold water and the salt. Allow the slices to soak for about 5 minutes to remove a bit of the starch, then drain them in a colander. Spread the slices out on paper towels and pat dry to remove any excess water.

In a deep, heavy skillet, heat 3 inches of oil over medium-high heat to 350°F. Line a plate with paper towels.

The oil is ready when a single piece of potato dropped in sizzles briskly but does not sputter violently. Carefully drop the sweet potato slices into the oil in batches, being careful not to overcrowd the skillet. Fry until crisp and golden brown. Transfer the chips to the paper towel–lined plate to drain. Sprinkle with a bit of salt while still hot, and serve with the dip.

NOTE: You can make both the dip and the chips ahead of time. The dip will keep nicely in the refrigerator for a couple of days. Fry the chips an hour or two before the party and spread them out evenly on a baking sheet so they stay crisp. The chips can be served at room temperature or warmed in a 200°F oven just before serving.

I've worked as a caterer for many years, and I've really learned what works at a party and what doesn't. Something that never fails is fried fish with a tangy sauce. It's just one of those magic combinations—flaky white fish enrobed in a crunchy, well-seasoned breading. Serve a little bowl of citrusy mayonnaise on the side, and people are transported to that seaside village of their dreams. When cut small and served elegantly, these fritters nod to good times and help to put guests in a sweet, nostalgic mood.

MASITAS DE MERO CON DIP DE LIMÓN
Grouper Fritters with Lemon Dip

SERVES 4

FOR THE DIP:
- 1 cup mayonnaise (page 106)
- 1 teaspoon grated lemon zest
- 1 tablespoon fresh lemon juice
- 1 tablespoon chopped fresh cilantro
  Kosher salt and freshly ground black pepper

FOR THE FISH:
- 2 grouper fillets, cut into 1½-inch strips
- 1 teaspoon adobo seasoning (page 144)
- 1 cup panko bread crumbs
- 1 cup all-purpose flour
  Vegetable oil, for deep-frying

MAKE THE DIP: In a small bowl, combine all of the ingredients and stir well. Cover and refrigerate for up to 24 hours.

MAKE THE FISH: Season the grouper on all sides with the adobo. In a medium bowl, stir together the panko and flour. Toss the seasoned grouper strips in the panko mixture.

In a large, heavy saucepan, heat 2 inches of vegetable oil over medium-high heat to 350°F. Line a plate with paper towels.

Working in batches, fry the grouper strips for 3 to 4 minutes, until golden brown. Using a slotted spoon, transfer the grouper to the paper towel–lined plate to drain. Serve immediately, with the dip on the side.

In every cafeteria on the island you will find *relleno de papa*, potato balls filled with ground beef, then fried and held under a giant, yellow warming lightbulb. People make them at home in the countryside as well, and we particularly enjoy them on Sundays. I like to play around with traditional recipes; here, instead of potato I use *apio*—a yellow root vegetable—with *tasajo*, a dried salted beef, as the filling. The flavors are a bit more complex, and it's a fun way to keep our native food interesting and vibrant.

RELLENO DE APIO DEL PAÍS CON TASAJO
Fried Root Vegetable Balls with Salted Beef

MAKES 12 CROQUETTES

5 pounds apio (see Notes), peeled and cut into 2-inch pieces
Kosher salt
2 pounds tasajo (see Notes)
2 tablespoons olive oil, plus more for your hands
1 yellow onion, diced
1 green cubanero pepper, diced
½ red bell pepper, diced
2 cloves garlic, mashed to a paste in a mortar
1 teaspoon dried oregano
1 tablespoon tomato paste
2 tablespoons chopped fresh cilantro
Vegetable oil, for deep-frying
All-purpose flour, for dredging

Put the apio in a medium saucepan and add enough water to cover by 1 inch. Bring to a boil and cook until tender, about 30 minutes. Remove from the heat, drain well, and mash immediately with a hand masher. Some lumps can remain. Lightly season the apio with salt, being careful not to oversalt, since the tasajo is salty. Let the apio mash cool completely.

Put the tasajo in a large saucepan and add enough water to cover by 4 to 6 inches. Bring to a boil, then reduce the heat, cover, and simmer until tender. This may take up to 4 hours. Add additional water if necessary to keep the tasajo completely submerged. Drain the tasajo and cut it into 1½-inch pieces so you don't have long strings. Shred the meat using your hands.

In a large saucepan, combine the olive oil and onion and cook over medium heat until the onion is translucent, about 5 minutes. Add the cubanero pepper, bell pepper, garlic, oregano, and tomato paste and continue to cook, stirring frequently, for 3 to 4 minutes. Add the shredded tasajo and cook for 10 minutes more. Taste for seasoning, add the cilantro, and add more salt if needed. Remove from the heat and let cool.

Lightly coat your hands with olive oil to prevent sticking. Divide the mashed apio into 12 equal portions and form each into a ball. Using your middle finger and index finger, start making a hole in the middle of the apio ball. Keep moving the ball until you have a big enough hole for 2 ounces of tasajo. Place the tasajo inside the apio and close the hole. Repeat with the remaining apio and tasajo. Set the filled balls on a plate or tray lined with waxed paper and refrigerate for at least 2 hours.

In a large, heavy saucepan, heat 2 inches of vegetable oil over high heat to 350°F. Line a plate with paper towels.

Dredge the balls in flour and tap off the excess. Carefully place them in the hot oil and fry for 3 to 4 minutes, until golden. Using a slotted spoon, transfer to the paper towel-lined plate to drain for 1 to 2 minutes, then serve.

NOTES: *Apio* is a starchy tuber that is used widely in the Caribbean (see page 27). It looks like a celery root, and is in fact part of the celery family, but has a much milder taste than celeriac. You can substitute another starchy tuber for this such as Idaho potatoes or taro.

You can find packaged *tasajo* in international markets, or you can substitute flat sheets of beef jerky.

PRIMER PLATO

First Course

Cool, vinegar-spiked salads are essential in the tropics. Our local ingredients cry out to be eaten fresh, with simple preparation. If you've only had mussels in the standard hot garlic-cream broth with crusty bread, this lively, bold dish will be a revelation. Served cold with a couple of *tostones* on the side, it is an elegant small plate. The mussels need to marinate overnight, so be sure to prepare this dish in advance.

MEJILLONES EN ESCABECHE
Marinated Mussels

SERVES 6 TO 8

6   pounds fresh live mussels, scrubbed and debearded
2   cups dry white wine
4   bay leaves
½   cup extra-virgin olive oil
1   onion, finely chopped
4   cloves garlic, minced
1   teaspoon salt
⅔   cup apple cider vinegar
8   whole black peppercorns
     Chopped hard-boiled eggs, for garnish (optional)
     Fresh tender cilantro, for garnish
     Tostones (page 166), for serving

Rinse the mussels well with cold water, drain, and place them in a heavy saucepan. Add 1 cup of the wine and the bay leaves. Cover and cook over medium heat, stirring occasionally, until the mussels begin to open, about 5 minutes. Drain in a colander over a bowl and discard any mussels that didn't open. Let the mussels cool, then remove the meat from the shells. Discard the shells and set the mussels aside.

In a heavy saucepan, heat the oil over medium heat. Add the onion, garlic, and salt. Cook until the onion is translucent, about 5 minutes. Add the vinegar, peppercorns, and the remaining 1 cup wine and bring to a boil. Reduce the heat to low and simmer for about 5 minutes. Remove from the heat and let cool, then pour into a bowl. Gently stir in the mussels, coating them completely with the liquid, then cover and refrigerate overnight.

Garnish with the hard-boiled eggs and cilantro and serve cold, with the tostones alongside.

This salad is one of my favorite flavor combinations and one that I learned to appreciate when I was working at New York's Le Bernardin in 1992, when there was a dish on the menu that incorporated white beans and fresh sardines. Growing up in Puerto Rico, I was raised with sardines and also white beans, but I had never tried them together until then. I have taken that flavor combination and put my touch on it with some local ingredients, but whenever I make this salad, great memories of living and working in New York come rushing back to me.

ENSALADA DE HABICHUELAS BLANCAS CON SARDINAS
White Bean Salad with Fresh Sardines

SERVES 4

2   cups fresh white beans, or 1½ cups dried white beans soaked in cold water overnight and drained

½   cup plus 3 tablespoons extra-virgin olive oil

2   tablespoons chopped shallot

1   tablespoon diced ají dulce pepper (see page 41)

2   tablespoons diced carrot

1   teaspoon apple cider vinegar

1   teaspoon fresh lemon juice

½   teaspoon kosher salt, plus more for sprinkling

½   teaspoon freshly ground black pepper

½   teaspoon chopped fresh oregano, plus whole sprigs for garnish

½   teaspoon chopped fresh basil

4   fresh sardines (see Note), cleaned

In a large pot, combine the beans with 4 cups water and bring to a boil; cook for about 25 minutes, or until tender (soaked dried beans will take longer). Drain the beans and plunge them into a bowl of ice water to stop the cooking process. Drain the beans again.

In a large bowl, combine the beans with ½ cup of the olive oil, the shallot, ají dulce, carrot, vinegar, lemon juice, salt, black pepper, and herbs and mix well. Cover and refrigerate until ready to serve.

Using the back of a knife, gently remove the scales from the sardines (but do not skin them) and carve out two fillets from each sardine. In a nonstick skillet, heat the remaining 3 tablespoons olive oil over medium-high heat. Sauté the sardine fillets, skin side down, for about 40 seconds, or until the flesh starts to turn opaque. Immediately remove from the heat and sprinkle lightly with salt.

To serve, distribute the white bean salad evenly among four serving plates and place two sardine fillets on top of each serving. Garnish with oregano sprigs.

NOTE: While this recipe gives instructions for using whole sardines, you can use fresh sardine fillets, which are available from many seafood and specialty grocers. We do not recommend canned sardines because the texture is so different.

We love pork with crisp skin here in Puerto Rico, and for us it is not difficult to find really good slow-cooked pork to purchase and take home to use in various recipes or to make sandwiches. Here, succulent pork, with a bit of the skin mixed in, is stuffed into what we call *criollo* bread. The bread is similar to Cuban bread or little baguettes—crusty on the outside but soft on the inside. You could use the pork leftover from the suckling pig on page 158, or the pork shoulder in the Pastelón de Lechón on page 120 for this, or you can use slow-cooked pork from a good local barbecue restaurant if you like. This recipe is inspired by our traditional pork sandwiches, but because I am so in love with Vietnamese bành mí, I have also mixed in a little of that great Asian combo of acid and heat with the pineapple jam and spicy mayo.

EMPAREDADO DE LECHÓN CON JALEA DE PIÑA
Pork Sandwich with Pineapple Jam

SERVES 2

2   (4½-inch) loaves freshly baked criollo bread from a Spanish panadería (or small hoagie rolls, Cuban rolls, or baguettes)

4   tablespoons spicy mayo (page 28), made with Sriracha sauce instead of pique

2   tablespoons pineapple jam (page 213)

2   (¼-inch-thick) slabs (lengthwise slices) seedless cucumber Kosher salt

2   tablespoons olive oil

2   (½-inch-thick) slices slow-cooked pork with crisp skin

2   leaves lechuga del país, or Bibb lettuce

Preheat the oven to 375°F.

Place the two loaves of bread in the oven for 2 minutes. Remove the bread from the oven and with the palm of your hand, press the loaves hard against a cutting board. Using a long, serrated knife, cut each loaf in half horizontally. Spread 1 tablespoon of the spicy mayo on the cut side of each bread slice. On one of the slices of each loaf, spread 1 tablespoon of the pineapple jam. Lay a slab of cucumber on top of the pineapple jam and sprinkle with a little salt.

In a small nonstick skillet, heat the oil over medium-high heat and heat the two slices of pork on both sides, about 1 minute per side. Dab the pork slices a bit with a paper towel to remove excess oil, and place one piece on each of the slices of bread with the cucumber and pineapple jam along with some of the crisp pork skin. Add the lettuce and close the sandwiches. Serve immediately.

LECHÓN

Some call it "roasted suckling pig" some call it Puerto Rican barbecue,
but no matter what you call it, *lechón* is always delicious.

There are entire streets dedicated to shops that specialize in *lechón*. The shops are called *lechoneras*, and each one features its version of suckling pig, roasted whole, on a rotating spit over smoldering wood coals. This method of slowly turning the pig over low, steady heat results in very moist, evenly cooked flesh and what some consider the most important part—crisp skin.

The *lechoneras* in Guavate, which is an area within the town of Cayey, are famous all over Puerto Rico. All along the main road, called *La Ruta del Lechón*, you will find kiosks and restaurants featuring this delicacy. Some have just one or two rotating spits for the pigs and some will have many more. But my favorite *lechonera* is located in a different area, Aguas Buenas, just a half hour from San Juan. Here, set among the green hills, is La Ranchera, the restaurant run by my friend Luis "Apa" Ramos. A third-generation pitmaster, he has emerged as sort of a *lechón* rock star over the last few years and has been featured on television shows and in print—he's also made a few trips to cook in the States. He has even cooked at New York's Le Bernardin, alongside our mutual friend Chef Eric Ripert. Apa has multiple pits for roasting the pigs, which are sourced locally. Aside from wanting to source products as close to home as possible, Apa knows that the pigs raised on the island are fed a lush diet of the same fruits, vegetables, and grains that we all eat here. The pigs raised in Puerto Rico taste different from imported ones and are therefore part of the flavor profile of *lechón*.

Preparing a pig for the spit is hard work. The pigs used are generally around three months old, around one hundred pounds (so they are not literally "suckling pigs"). First, the *lechón* master prepares a marinade mixture that consists of mashed garlic and salt and often ají dulce, *culantro*, and oregano. Small cuts, about an inch deep (but not puncturing the meat), are made in the skin and fat of the exterior so that the garlic and herb mixture permeates within. Then the pig is allowed to marinate for two days. The *lechón* master then secures the pig to the spit and sets it upon a rig outfitted with a motor that keeps it spinning slowly over charcoal made from three different kinds of Puerto Rican hardwood. Cooking time ranges from five to six hours. Sometimes many pigs will be spinning in these cinderblock pits, all by the same motor, with the spits connected by repurposed bicycle chains. It's a very efficient way of cooking a lot of food at one time. In the busy holiday season, Apa may sell up to 100 pigs a day. His work is done in a smoke-filled area, but when Apa puts on his favorite classic salsa crooner music from the '40s and '50s, the workspace becomes a dreamy place where it seems like the pigs are twirling to the music. After about five hours, each pig is removed from the spit, the head is cut off, and the meat is cut into chunks with a large machete-like knife. It's a sensational experience to listen to the music, smell the roasted pig, and laugh with Apa while he cracks jokes and wields a giant machete to cut up the whole pig. To say the very least, *lechón* is much more than a food—it is a piece of our culture, the essence of eating in Puerto Rico.

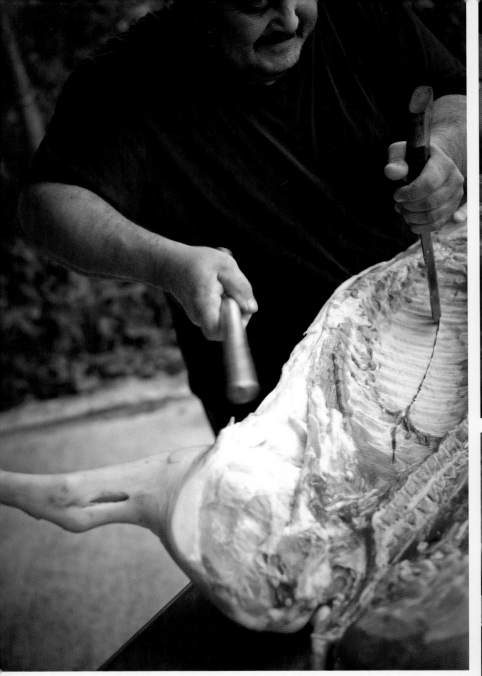

Clockwise from top left: Apa uses a machete and a mallet to butcher the pig before seasoning and cooking; the seasoning mix to be rubbed onto the meat; the pig on a spit; cutting up the roast pig; a serving platter of *lechón* with the essential, candy-like crispy skin known as *cuerito*; *gandinga*, a stew that makes use of the organ meats from the pig.

Pigeon peas are a tropical green pea that made their way to Puerto Rico via the African slave trade and have grown very well here ever since. Pigeon peas have a very green, fresh taste and are a versatile staple in the Puerto Rican kitchen. Many people have them growing in their backyard gardens, and they grow so well that it's not uncommon to visit someone's house and be sent home with bags of fresh-picked or frozen peas.

SOPA DE GANDULES CON BOLLITAS DE PLÁTANO

Pigeon Pea Soup with Green Plantain Dumplings

SERVES 6 TO 8

2 green plantains
⅓ cup olive oil
6 cloves garlic, mashed to a paste in a mortar
1 large yellow onion, chopped
3 red bell peppers, seeded and diced
2 tablespoons tomato paste
4 fresh culantro leaves, minced
½ cup chopped fresh cilantro, plus more for garnish
1 tablespoon dried oregano
1 pound frozen or fresh green pigeon peas
1 bone-in smoked ham hock
   Kosher salt and freshly ground black pepper

Peel the plantains and grate them on the next-to-smallest holes of a box grater. Scoop out ½ tablespoon portions of the shredded plantain and form them into balls. Set aside on a plate lined with waxed paper.

In a soup pot, heat the oil over medium-high heat. Add the garlic, onion, bell peppers, tomato paste, culantro, cilantro, and oregano and sauté, stirring continuously, for about 2 minutes. Add the pigeon peas and stir again until well combined. Cook for about 2 minutes more, then add 3 quarts water and the ham hock. Bring to a boil over high heat and add the plantain dumplings. Reduce the heat to medium-low and simmer for 30 minutes.

Season with salt and pepper to taste, and serve in individual bowls, garnished with a little chopped cilantro.

NOTE: The bollitas are a sort of dumpling made by seasoning grated green plantains, forming the mixture into balls, and simmering them in the pea soup.

Ñame (pronounced "nya-may") is one of the largest root vegetables grown on the island (see page 27). The taste and texture is less starchy than *apio* and cassava and is therefore easier to blend into a creamier texture. Here, the combination of one of our regional vegetables topped with a dollop of sofrito creates a unique taste that could only be Puerto Rican. If you have trouble finding *ñame* in international markets, you can substitute Yukon gold potatoes.

CREMA DE ÑAME CON SOFRITO
Creamy Root Vegetable Soup with Sofrito

SERVES 6

4   pounds ñame or Yukon gold potatoes, peeled and diced
7   cups water or chicken broth or a combination
1   yellow onion, finely diced
4   cloves garlic, mashed to a paste in a mortar
1   teaspoon kosher salt, plus more as needed
1   teaspoon freshly ground black pepper, plus more as needed
    Sofrito (page 40), for garnish

In a large pot, combine the ñame, water and/or broth, onion, garlic, salt, and pepper and bring to a boil. Reduce the heat to medium-low and cook until the ñame is very tender, about 45 minutes. Let cool.

Working in batches, transfer the mixture to a blender and blend until smooth. Return to the pot and reheat over medium-low heat. Taste and adjust the seasonings.

Serve hot, with a dollop of sofrito for garnish.

Cooking like a chef means utilizing every opportunity to enhance flavor. The peels of onions, stems of parsley, shrimp shells, and bones that might get thrown away by an amateur cook are treasured by a professional. Long ago, home cooks knew what to do with these ingredients, but as our lives have become more "convenient" we have lost a little bit of that need to save and savor every usable element. This broth uses the bones of red snapper—a fish that is abundant and native to the waters around Puerto Rico. The next time you cook a fish like a red snapper, save the bones by wrapping them and tossing them in the freezer. When you want to make soup, throw the bones in a pot with some basic aromatics like onion, carrot, and celery, and you have a beautiful, homemade fish stock from which to start.

CALDO DE PESCADO CON CALABAZA
Fish Broth with Pumpkin

SERVES 4 TO 6

Bones of 2 red snappers
1 white onion, quartered
1 carrot, quartered
1 celery rib, quartered
4 cloves garlic, mashed to a paste in a mortar
½ tablespoon dried oregano
1 tablespoon kosher salt, plus more as needed
4 sprigs fresh cilantro
1½ pounds calabaza (see page 27, or fresh pumpkin), cut into 1-inch pieces, half peeled, half with skin
Fresh culantro leaves, for garnish
Fresh oregano sprigs, for garnish

In a large pot, combine the fish bones, onion, carrot, celery, garlic, oregano, salt, and cilantro and cover with water. Bring to a simmer over medium-high heat, reduce the heat to medium, and cook for about 30 minutes. Remove from the heat and let cool.

Pour the broth through a fine-mesh sieve set over a large bowl. Discard the solids and return the liquid to the pot. Bring to a simmer over medium heat. Add the pumpkin chunks and cook until the pumpkin is tender, about 20 minutes.

Taste and adjust the salt, then transfer to individual bowls and garnish with the culantro leaves and oregano sprigs. Serve very hot.

Colorful and cheerful, this salad is filled with iconic flavors of the island. Its sweetness makes it a great starter for a summer lunch or brunch. Fresh coconut can be found everywhere here—sold in markets and on street corners at every turn. Once you master opening a fresh coconut, you will find that there is no contest when comparing canned or dried coconut to the taste of fresh coconut water, the refreshing, meaty flesh, and the coconut milk that one fruit provides.

ENSALADA DE GUINEOS Y PIÑA EN LECHE DE COCO, LIMÓN Y MIEL

Fruit Salad with Fresh Coconut Milk and Honey

MAKES 4 TO 6 SERVINGS

Juice of 1 lemon
3 tablespoons honey
1 cup fresh coconut milk (page 187)
4 cups cubed fresh pineapple
3 bananas, cut into ½-inch rounds
Fresh mint, for garnish

In a large bowl, whisk together the lemon juice, honey, and coconut milk. Add the pineapple and banana and stir gently to combine. Cover and refrigerate for up to 1 hour, until ready to serve. Garnish with mint and serve chilled.

To say that this recipe is an ecstatic combination of Puerto Rican flavors is not an overstatement. Even the colors are joyful. Beloved pork belly plays well beside fresh, cold chunks of fruit and the mild taste and texture of queso de hoja, a cow's-milk cheese similar to string cheese (you can substitute any medium-firm, mild white cheese). The pork belly needs to chill for at least 3 hours before being roasted, so be sure to begin the recipe well in advance of when you plan to serve it.

ENSALADA DE PANZA DE CERDO CON SANDÍAS, MANGÓ Y QUESO DE HOJA

Pork Belly Salad with Watermelon, Mango, and Puerto Rican Cheese

SERVES 6 TO 8

FOR THE PORK BELLY:
- 1 (3-pound) slab skinless pork belly
- 1 teaspoon kosher salt
- 1 teaspoon granulated sugar

FOR THE DRESSING:
- 1 cup olive oil
- 1 teaspoon minced shallot
- 2 tablespoons apple cider vinegar
- ¼ cup fresh orange juice
- 1 teaspoon honey
  Kosher salt and freshly ground black pepper

FOR THE SALAD:
- 1 pound arugula
- 5 ounces lechuga del país (local lettuce) or Boston lettuce, torn into 1½-inch-wide pieces
- 1 small seedless watermelon (about 2 pounds), rind removed, flesh cut into ½-inch pieces
- 2 mangoes, peeled and finely diced
- 8 ounces queso de hoja or other white cow's-milk cheese, cut into ½-inch pieces
- 1 tablespoon olive oil

MAKE THE PORK BELLY: Place the pork belly in a roasting pan. Combine the salt and sugar in a small bowl and rub the mixture all over the meat. Discard any excess salt-and-sugar mixture. Cover the pan with plastic wrap and refrigerate for at least 6 hours and up to 24 hours.

Preheat the oven to 450°F.

Remove any excess liquid that has accumulated in the bottom of the roasting pan. Make sure the pork belly is fat side up in the pan, then roast for 1 hour, basting the pork with rendered fat from the pan at the halfway point, until it's golden brown. Reduce the oven temperature to 250°F and cook for another 1 hour, or until the pork belly is tender. Remove the pan from the oven and transfer the pork belly to a large plate. Let cool slightly. Wrap the pork belly in plastic wrap and refrigerate until chilled and firm enough to cut easily, about 2 hours. (You can prepare the pork up to 2 days in advance.)

MAKE THE DRESSING: While the pork belly is chilling, in a small bowl, slowly whisk together all of the ingredients in a small bowl until well combined. The dressing doesn't need to be emulsified.

MAKE THE SALAD: In a large bowl, combine the arugula and lettuce. Add the watermelon and mangoes and toss well. Add the cheese and the dressing and mix again.

Just before serving, cut the chilled pork belly into 1-inch cubes. Heat the oil in a nonstick skillet over medium-high heat. Add the pork belly and sauté for 2 to 3 minutes on each side until golden brown, crisp, and dark in some areas. Transfer to a paper towel–lined plate to drain for 30 seconds.

Add the pork belly pieces to the bowl with the salad and mix until well combined. Serve immediately, while the pork belly is hot.

To me, roasted beets are like the taste of the earth itself. The crisp, raw edge that raw beets have is mellowed by roasting, and the natural sugars are brought out just enough to deepen the flavor. I make this nouveau classic salad my own by adding a crumbling of our local *queso del país*—a fresh white cheese with mild tang. This delicious yet humble cheese features the milk from dairies of the interior of Puerto Rico. It is quite versatile because of its mild flavor and semisoft texture. If you can't find Puerto Rican white cheese, you can substitute ricotta salata or goat cheese crumbles.

ENSALADA DE REMOLACHAS ASADAS CON ADEREZO DE MANZANA
Roasted Beet Salad with Apple Vinaigrette

SERVES 6 TO 8

4   medium beets, trimmed
3   tablespoons plus ¾ cup Spanish olive oil
¼   cup apple cider vinegar
1   teaspoon granulated sugar
1   tablespoon finely chopped shallot
     Kosher salt and freshly ground black pepper
3   tablespoons crumbled queso del país (fresh white cheese)
     Fresh cilantro leaves, for garnish

Preheat the oven to 375°F.

Coat the beets lightly with the 3 tablespoons of the oil. Place them on a baking sheet and roast until cooked through and tender, 45 to 60 minutes. Let cool, then peel the beets and finely dice them.

To make the vinaigrette, whisk together the vinegar, sugar, shallot, and salt and pepper in a bowl. While whisking, slowly drizzle in the remaining ¾ cup oil until emulsified.

Place the beets in a large bowl, pour the vinaigrette over them, and toss to coat the beets. Spoon the beets onto a serving plate, top with the cheese, and garnish with the cilantro leaves. Serve immediately.

This beautiful salad features two ingredients that are common in Puerto Rico but offer something exotic and unfamiliar to cooks outside of the Caribbean. *Apio* (page 27) is sometimes confused with standard celery root. Even though they are in the same family, they are very different. The *apio* root is starchy, more like a potato, and has a much milder flavor than celery root. Sour oranges (sometimes called Seville oranges) are in the same family as the common sweet orange but have a tart and slightly bitter tang and a different aroma—closer to a lime than an orange (page 208). They are becoming easier to find in the States, and if you do see some, grab them and start experimenting with the juice. If you can't find sour oranges, use equal parts regular orange juice and lime juice.

ENSALADA DE CALAMARES CON APIO DEL PAÍS EN ADEREZO DE NARANJA AGRIA

Calamari Salad with Puerto Rican Root Vegetable in Sour Orange Dressing

SERVES 6 TO 8

4   pounds apio, peeled and cut into 1-inch pieces
2   tablespoons kosher salt, or more to taste
16 baby squid (calamari), cleaned
4   bay leaves
    Juice of 2 sour oranges
1   cup extra-virgin olive oil
2   tablespoons finely chopped fresh cilantro

In a large saucepan, combine the apio and salt and add enough water to cover by 1 inch. Bring the water to a boil and cook until the apio is tender, about 30 minutes. Drain the apio and transfer to a bowl of ice water to stop the cooking. Let cool for 3 to 5 minutes, then drain again.

In a separate saucepan, combine the calamari and bay leaves and add enough water to cover. Bring to a boil and cook for 3 to 5 minutes. Drain the calamari, discarding the bay leaves, and transfer to a bowl of cold water to stop the cooking. Let cool, then drain.

Cut the calamari crosswise into ¼-inch pieces and put them in a large bowl. Add the apio, orange juice, oil, and cilantro and stir to combine. Taste and adjust the seasoning. Refrigerate until ready to serve. Serve chilled.

An ancient vine bearing large, pear-shaped squash, the *chayote* was once enjoyed by Aztecs, Mayas, and other Indian tribes of the tropics. Delicious raw or cooked, they grow well only in warm climates, and the vines are lively and prolific in Puerto Rico. In the States, you might hear them referred to as mirliton, which is what the Creole and Cajun cooks of Louisiana call them, or christophene. There are a few varieties of chayote—some with smooth, white or pale green skin and others with sharp spines on them. They all have a similar mild taste with a crunchy texture, but for this recipe purchase the white variety if given the choice (pictured, page 26), as it takes better to boiling whereas the green variety lends itself more to being eaten raw.

ENSALADA DE CHAYOTE CON ADEREZO DE ALMENDRAS ROSTIZADAS
Chayote Salad with Roasted Almond Dressing

SERVES 4

½ cup sliced almonds
3   chayote squash
2   tablespoons kosher salt,
    or more to taste
¾ cup extra-virgin olive oil
1   tablespoon apple cider vinegar
3   tablespoons chopped fresh
    cilantro

Preheat the oven to 350°F.

Spread the almonds out on a rimmed baking sheet and toast them in the oven until fragrant, about 6 minutes. Set aside to cool.

Peel the chayotes, cut them in half, and scoop out the center pit and fibers with a spoon. Cut the chayote flesh into ½-inch cubes. Fill a saucepan about halfway with water and bring to a boil. Add the chayote and 1 tablespoon of the salt and cook for 10 minutes, or until the chayote is fork-tender. Fill a large bowl with ice water. Drain the chayote and immediately plunge into the ice water to stop the cooking. Drain again and put in a bowl.

Toss the cooked chayote with the remaining 1 tablespoon salt and let stand for about 15 minutes, stirring occasionally, to help pull additional water out of the chayote. Drain again, spread the chayote pieces on a few paper towels, and let drain for a few minutes.

Transfer to a large bowl and add the oil, vinegar, cilantro, and toasted almonds. Add salt to taste, cover, and refrigerate for up to 1 hour. Serve chilled.

PLAZA DEL MERCADO DE SANTURCE

"La Placita" is all you have to say to a Sanjuanero and they immediately know you are referring to the Plaza del Mercado de Santurce.

Located in the middle of a neighborhood within walking distance of the bustling tourist district of Condado, this area is a beautiful view into what being a resident of San Juan is like. The vibe is a mix of old-school, working-class borough and bohemian hipster enclave (the feeling of this community is what drew me to it as the location for my restaurant Santaella). The colorful cottages built in the late 1930s and '40s reflect a typical homeowner's dream of tree-lined streets, single-family houses with small yards and sitting porches. The neighborhood has moved in and out of favor and fallen into a state of disrepair at times, but it is enjoying an upward phase currently as young professionals, artists, and small businesses move in and boost the economic complexion and cultural energy. At the heart of the neighborhood is Mercado de Santurce, a century-old produce market housed in a grand building in the middle of the neighborhood plaza. Large open doors on all sides of the mercado keep the air moving, allowing the smells of farm-fresh produce to waft out along with the sounds of lively conversation and business transactions. Inside, stalls filled with pallets loaded with stalks of plantains, bananas, and other tropical fruits and vegetables are tended to by vendors who display them with pride and a competitive spirit. Some of the vendors are farmers, but many of them are distributors or middlemen who source the produce and then set up stalls in the large market, creating great choice and lively commerce. There are so many stalls filled with the same produce that one wonders how they sell it all, but home cooks and professionals alike shop at this market and keep the turnover heavy. Other vendors in the market sell meat, cheese, culinary and medicinal herbs, and prepared foods such as empanadillas and sandwiches.

Around the perimeter of La Placita are walk-up bars, sandwich shops, cafés, and restaurants, along with shops and stalls selling fresh blended fruit smoothies, or *batidas*, in combinations like papaya and coconut water, or mango with milk—or even ice cream. At night, especially on the weekends, the entire plaza turns into a street party. The music is loud, and there are happy people eating, drinking, and dancing out on the sidewalks; a visit to La Placita after dark is a great way to experience the Puerto Rican love of parties.

Clockwise from top left: The open-air building was constructed in 1910 in the *criollo* neoclassic style; plantains and bananas hang on their branches; green bananas are delivered from a local farm; a nearby Santeria shop specializes in potions of all kinds; green bananas.

The crystal-blue waters of the Caribbean provide a clear lens through which snorkelers may view the rainbow of sea life that lives below the waves. It also provides fishermen and divers a clean landscape for catching and collecting fish, shellfish, and spiny lobsters. When we want to see what is being brought in fresh from the Caribbean Sea, we head to Guanica on the south side of the island. Because there are many fishermen working out of this harbor, there is a great opportunity to buy directly from them such local favorites as snapper, ladyfish, and conch. The pink spiral shells of the conch are perhaps the most coveted prize of shell collectors, but do they know about the sweet, briny meat of the mollusk that makes its home inside? Fresh conch meat can be sliced thin and eaten completely raw with just salt and maybe some citrus or vinegar, but frozen conch is easier to find and quite good. The conch in this recipe is cooked for an hour to ensure that it is tender before being tossed into this fresh, peppery salad.

ENSALADA DE CARRUCHO
Conch Salad

SERVES 4 TO 6

3   pounds fresh or frozen conch meat
3   tablespoons kosher salt, plus more as needed
10 bay leaves
2   cups olive oil
2   cups diced white onions
1   red bell pepper, finely diced
1   green cubanero pepper, finely diced
6   small ají dulce peppers (see page 41), finely diced
1   tablespoon apple cider vinegar
2   tablespoons fresh lime juice
3   tablespoons finely chopped fresh cilantro
2   cloves garlic, mashed to a paste in a mortar
10 green olives, pitted and chopped
    Freshly ground black pepper

In a large pot, combine the conch, salt, and bay leaves and add enough water to cover. Bring to a boil, reduce the heat to medium, and cook until the conch is tender, about 1 hour. Drain and submerge the conch in a bowl filled with ice water to stop the cooking. Drain again and, with a knife, scrape all of the yellowish skin that remains from the conch. Cut the white flesh into ¼-inch-thick slices. Let cool, then cover and put in the refrigerator.

In a medium saucepan, heat 3 tablespoons of the oil over low heat. Add the onions and sauté until translucent, about 7 minutes. Remove from the heat and let cool.

In a medium bowl, combine the remaining oil, sautéed onions, conch, all of the peppers, the vinegar, lime juice, cilantro, garlic, and olives and mix well. Taste and adjust the seasoning with salt and black pepper. Refrigerate until ready to serve.

There is much discussion these days about the sustainability and safety of seafood. It can be very confusing, with conflicting information bombarding us constantly. A fish that might be endangered in one part of the world could be thriving in another. Thankfully, one of my favorite fishes, the red snapper, is healthy and abundant in the waters of the Atlantic, the Caribbean, and the Gulf of Mexico. It is a gorgeous, mild-flavored fish that is suitable for every treatment—even raw, as in this elegant crudo and avocado dish.

CRUDO DE CHILLO CON AGUACATE EN MAYONESA DE RECAO SERVIDO CON MARIQUITA DE PLÁTANO

Snapper Crudo with Avocado, Culantro Mayonnaise, and Plantain Chips

SERVES 4 TO 6

2	skinless red snapper fillets
1	teaspoon kosher salt, plus more as needed
2	tablespoons extra-virgin olive oil, plus more as needed
½	teaspoon fresh lime juice
1	green plantain
2	tablespoons vegetable oil
1	avocado, peeled and cut into ¼-inch cubes
1	fresh culantro leaf, minced
2	tablespoons mayonnaise (recipe follows)

4 to 6 teaspoons eggs vinaigrette (recipe follows)

Finely dice the fish. In a medium bowl, combine the fish, salt, olive oil, and lime juice, and mix well.

Peel the green plantain and cut it lengthwise with a mandoline into paper-thin slices.

In a saucepan, heat the vegetable oil over medium heat. Add the plantain slices and fry, turning, until crisp, about 4 minutes. Transfer to a paper towel–lined plate to drain briefly.

In a small bowl, season the avocado cubes with salt and olive oil. Divide the avocado among serving plates and top with the fish mixture. Stir the culantro into the mayonnaise. Place a dollop of the culantro mayo on top of the fish on each plate. Garnish with a fried plantain slice. Place 1 teaspoon of the eggs vinaigrette on the side of each plate and serve immediately.

EGGS VINAIGRETTE

MAKES ABOUT 6 TABLESPOONS

3	hard-boiled eggs
1	tablespoon extra-virgin olive oil
½	teaspoon sherry vinegar or apple cider vinegar
	Kosher salt

Cut the eggs in half, remove the yolks (discard or save them for another use), and finely dice the whites. In a small bowl, combine the egg whites, oil, and vinegar and season to taste with salt. Store, covered, in the refrigerator for up to 24 hours.

MAYONNAISE

MAKES ABOUT 1 CUP

1	large egg yolk, at room temperature
1½	tablespoons fresh lemon juice
1	tablespoon white wine vinegar
½	tablespoon Dijon mustard
	Kosher salt
¾	cup good-quality olive oil
¼	tablespoon freshly ground white pepper

Whisk together the egg yolk, lemon juice, vinegar, mustard, and a pinch of salt until well combined. Add the oil, just a few drops at a time at first, then in a thin stream, whisking continuously until the mixture begins to thicken. Add the white pepper and mix well. Taste and adjust the seasoning. Store in an airtight container in the refrigerator for up to 1 week.

A hearty plate of scrambled eggs and sausage is a great way to start the day, but using your own pork sausage takes it beyond your average, everyday breakfast. If you're making the homemade sausage, note that it needs to be started about five days in advance so it can cure; alternatively, you can substitute Spanish chorizo for the longaniza called for here.

HUEVOS REVUELTOS CON LONGANIZA Y CILANTRO
Scrambled Eggs with Longaniza Sausage and Cilantro

SERVES 6

3   homemade Pork Longaniza Sausage Links (recipe below)
15   large eggs
¼   cup heavy cream
¼   cup whole milk
1   clove garlic, mashed to a paste in a mortar
3   tablespoons cream cheese, at room temperature
½   tablespoon olive oil
½   tablespoon butter
1½   tablespoons chopped fresh cilantro

In a medium saucepan, bring 3 inches of water to a boil. Add the sausage links and boil for 1 minute. Remove from the water and let cool to room temperature, about 30 minutes. Cut the sausage links into small pieces and set aside.

In a medium bowl, combine the eggs, cream, milk, and garlic. Whisk until well combined. Add the cream cheese and whisk to combine.

In a nonstick skillet, heat the oil and butter over medium-high heat. Add the egg mixture and cook, stirring occasionally with a rubber spatula so the egg mixture doesn't stick, until the eggs begin to set but are still moist.

Meanwhile, in a separate skillet, sauté the sausage pieces over medium-high heat until browned. Add the sautéed sausage to the scrambled eggs and garnish with the chopped cilantro. Mix well and serve immediately.

PORK LONGANIZA SAUSAGE LINKS

MAKES 12 (3-INCH) LINKS

2   pounds ground pork
½   pound pork fat, finely diced
½   pound pork belly, finely diced
2   cloves garlic, mashed to a paste in a mortar
2   tablespoons annatto oil (page 000)
2   tablespoons white wine vinegar
2   tablespoons finely chopped fresh cilantro
1½   tablespoons kosher salt
1   tablespoon freshly ground black pepper
1   teaspoon smoked paprika
½   teaspoon dried oregano
½   teaspoon red pepper flakes
¼   teaspoon curing salt (salt and sodium nitrite, also known as InstaCure #1 or "pink salt")
        About 5 feet of natural sausage casings

In a large bowl, combine all the ingredients except the sausage casings and mix well to combine. Let the mixture stand, covered in the refrigerator, for 1 to 2 hours.

Fill the sausage casings using a stuffing machine or the sausage attachment on a stand mixer. (Alternatively, you can use a funnel—you will need another person to help you if you use this method.) Tie the ends of the filled casing with kitchen string. Twist the sausage every 5 inches or so to form the links.

Place the finished sausages on a plate or tray and let them cure and dry in the refrigerator, uncovered, for 4 or 5 days, turning them over once a day. Cook as directed in the recipe on page 19.

The verdant taste and sturdy texture of green bananas is showcased in a very unique way when they are pickled. While it might sound strange and exotic to many, this is a fairly common side dish in Puerto Rico, usually eaten around Christmastime. The rich, pork-heavy holiday recipes traditionally served during this time are brightened by cool, vinegary pickles on the plate. The pickles need to be refrigerated overnight, so be sure to prepare them well in advance of serving.

GUINEITOS EN ESCABECHE
Pickled Green Bananas

MAKES 8 TO 10 CUPS

2 cups whole milk
1 teaspoon kosher salt
10 large green bananas
1 pound yellow onions, cut into ⅛-inch-thick rounds
1 cup distilled white vinegar
4 cloves garlic, peeled
12 pimento-stuffed green olives, halved
10 whole black peppercorns
4 bay leaves
3 cups extra-virgin olive oil

In a caldero (see page 23, or use a Dutch oven or heavy sauce pan), combine 8 cups water, the milk, and the salt and bring to a boil over medium-high heat. Make a long lengthwise slit in each of the green bananas, but do not cut into the flesh of the fruit and do not peel. Add them to the milk mixture, and boil for about 20 minutes.

Meanwhile, put the onions, vinegar, garlic, olives, peppercorns, and bay leaves in a skillet. Pour the oil over the ingredients and set over low heat to cook until the onions are translucent but still a bit firm, about 45 minutes. Remove from the heat and let cool to room temperature.

Remove the green bananas from their cooking liquid and carefully peel off the skin. Cut the bananas into 1-inch pieces and place in a bowl; add the onion mixture and mix together. Cover and refrigerate overnight. Serve chilled or at room temperature.

**PLATOS
PRINCIPALES**
Main Dishes

The pork-eating cultures of the world understand and celebrate the beautiful qualities of each part of the animal. Trotters, or pig's feet, have a special way of turning sauces and broth silky and thick. Cooked for a long time, the meat from the trotters takes on a delightful, unusual texture and flavor. When I was a little boy I adored pig's feet. My mom used to make them all the time, and I would get the sticky, succulent sauce all over my little hands. It's a good memory and supplied me with the love of the deep complexity that pig's feet can bring to a dish. This recipe, with my addition of shrimp, reminds me of many of the complex Asian dishes that feature silky pork broth and lots of fresh herbs. It's a comforting memory for me but also an exotic plate to cook at home. I like to serve it with white rice (page 132) or tostones (page 166).

CAMARONES SALTEADOS EN CALDO DE PATITAS DE CERDO
Sautéed Shrimp in Pig's Feet Broth

SERVES 6

FOR THE BROTH:

6   salted or fresh pig's feet (see Note)
2   yellow onions, quartered
4   cloves garlic, mashed to a paste in a mortar

FOR THE SHRIMP:

18 extra-large tiger shrimp, peeled and deveined
¼   cup grapeseed oil
1   teaspoon kosher salt
¼   cup chopped fresh mint
¼   cup chopped fresh chives
3   tablespoons chopped fresh dill
6   sprigs fresh oregano
¼   cup chopped fresh cilantro

MAKE THE BROTH: Rinse salted pig's feet very well to remove the salt; there's no need to rinse fresh pig's feet. In a stockpot, combine the pig's feet, onions, and garlic and add enough water to cover. Bring to a boil, then reduce the heat to low and cook for 1½ to 2 hours, until the pig's feet are tender. Skim foam and impurities off the surface of the broth occasionally during cooking. Taste the broth; if it seems too salty, add more water. Pour through a colander set over a large pot and discard the solids. Reheat the broth to serve with the shrimp or allow the broth to cool, then cover and store in the refrigerator for up to 3 days or in the freezer for up to 1 month.

MAKE THE SHRIMP: Cut the shrimp lengthwise into 2 pieces each. In a large skillet, heat the oil over high heat. Add the shrimp and sauté for 1½ minutes. Sprinkle with the salt, mint, chives, and dill. Toss to mix well. Add the shrimp and herb mixture to the hot broth.

Serve immediately, ladled into bowls with a sprinkle of cilantro and an oregano sprig on each serving.

NOTE: Pig's feet can be ordered from your butcher, but many markets carry them regularly. They are easy to find in the South and in international markets. Sometimes they come with a thick layer of salt on them—this is typical in Puerto Rico. If yours are salted, be sure to rinse them well before cooking.

Preparing beef stew is, for me, a holistic experience: the sound of the beef searing in the pan to obtain its initial mahogany coating, followed by the fragrant, tannic steam that rises when the red wine is poured, and the hour and a half or so of deep simmering aroma that fills the house as it cooks. Finally, ladling the chunks of tender meat, coated in their unctuous gravy, over pork rind–studded rice is the moment of satisfaction. Beef stew is beloved all over the world. The basics of the recipe connect us through the same happy experience of loving preparation, slow anticipation, and joyful resolve.

CARNE GUISADA SERVIDA CON ARROZ CON TOCINO
Beef Stew with Pork Rind Rice

SERVES 4 TO 6

2   pounds beef top round steak, trimmed and cut into 1-inch chunks
1   tablespoon adobo seasoning (page 144)
1   tablespoon vegetable oil
¼   cup sofrito (page 40)
6   fresh cilantro leaves
2   tablespoons tomato paste
½   cup red wine
½   teaspoon dried oregano, crushed
2   bay leaves
1   tablespoon kosher salt, or more to taste
½   pound carrots, peeled and cut into ½-inch rounds
      Pork Rind Rice (recipe follows)

Season the meat with the adobo. In a large pot, heat the oil over high heat until shimmering. Add the beef and cook until seared on all sides, about 5 minutes. Add the sofrito, cilantro, and tomato paste and cook, stirring, until the meat is browned, 4 to 5 minutes. Pour in 4 cups water and the wine and bring to a boil. Reduce the heat to low and add the oregano, bay leaves, salt, and carrots. Cover and cook for about 1 hour, until the meat is tender. Uncover and cook until the liquid has reduced and thickened, about 15 minutes.

Taste and adjust the seasoning with salt. Serve with the pork rind rice.

PORK RIND RICE

SERVES 4 TO 6

¼   cup extra-virgin olive oil
1   cup fresh or cured pork rinds (see page 116), finely diced
3   cups water
2   cups medium- or short-grain white rice
2   teaspoons kosher salt

In a medium caldero (or a Dutch oven or heavy saucepan), heat the oil over medium-high heat. Add the pork rinds and sauté, stirring to keep them from sticking. Add the rice, stirring continuously for about 1 minute to coat the rice with oil. Add 3 cups water and the salt and bring to a boil. Reduce the heat to medium, stir, and cover the pot; cook for 10 to 15 minutes, then stir again. Cover the pot again and cook for 10 to 15 minutes more, until the rice is tender and all the water has been absorbed. Serve hot.

PORK RIND

Sheets of *chicharrón*, fried pork skin, are ubiquitous on the island.

We enjoy eating *chicharrón*, which some may call cracklings, as a snack, but we also like to crumble them up as a salty, crisp ingredient in many of our recipes. Perhaps the most familiar, and possibly the most famous dish that utilizes them is *mofongo*, in which green plantains are fried and then mashed in a wooden mortar and pestle with garlic and very crisp *chicharrón*. The mixture is typically pressed to take on the form of the mortar and pestle, turned out onto a plate, and served hot. The *mofongo* with spiny lobster on page 147 is an elevated version of the simple, homey *mofongo* that is built on the traditional green plantain and *chicharrón* mixture. *Chicharrón* are so important here that Bayamón—the second largest city in Puerto Rico—is known as *El Pueblo del Chicharrón*.

Puerto Rican *chicharrón* are not the same product as the packages of puffy fried pork rinds that you might see at a convenience store in the States. The skins that we make here are cut from the belly and sometimes have just a bit of lean meat left on. When the belly chunks are cooked, some of the fat will render out and the skin will become crisp with a tiny bit of underlying chewiness. *Chicharrón* can be purchased from the many *lechoneras* on the island or from the markets or kiosks that sell food products. (No one really makes them at home.) If you're lucky enough to live near an international or Latin market, *chicharrón* will be quite easy to find, or you can order them online. Check local butcher shops and farmers' markets, too.

Another pork skin product important here is *tocino* (pictured, at right in *arroz con tocino*). Usually taken from the back of the pig, *tocino* is salt cured, which preserves it and concentrates the flavor. Since it has less moisture than *chicharrón*, *tocino* puffs up less when it is cooked, giving it a more dense, toothsome quality.

Linda worked as a waitress at the twenty-four-hour cafeteria that my father owned when I was about nine years old. She was very nice and was always there to greet me when I would show up for lunch. Each Friday the restaurant would prepare *serenata*—a mixed codfish salad with root vegetables, green bananas, avocados, and hard-boiled eggs, among other fresh ingredients. It was complex but fresh, and both Linda and I loved it; I made her promise to wait for me to arrive from school so we could eat together. Spending time at my father's place, meeting all the people who worked there, and observing the rhythm of a restaurant instilled a love of the work in me and supplied great memories. To this day I make a *serenata* at Santaella every Friday for the lunch menu. Begin preparing this dish at least a day in advance of when you plan to serve it, as the salt cod requires a long rest in the fridge.

SERENATA DE BACALAO CON AGUACATE Y VIANDAS

Codfish Salad with Avocado and Root Vegetables

SERVES 4 TO 6

1 gallon milk
1½ pounds salt cod (bacalao)
½ pound yautia (see page 27), peeled and cut into 1-inch pieces
½ pound batata (see page 27) or sweet potatoes, peeled and cut into 1-inch pieces
6 green bananas, peeled and cut into 1-inch pieces
1 red onion, thinly sliced
3 tomatoes, diced
1½ cups extra-virgin olive oil (preferably Spanish)
4 handfuls fresh local salad greens
2 avocados, peeled and diced
3 hard-boiled eggs, sliced

In a large, deep bowl, combine the milk and 1 gallon water and submerge the codfish in the liquid; cover and let soak in the refrigerator for 2 days or at least overnight. (The milk helps make the fish flaky.)

Bring a large pot of water to a boil. Add the yautia, sweet potato, and green bananas and cook until tender but not falling apart, about 20 minutes. Check each vegetable with a knife and as soon as pieces become tender, remove them with a slotted spoon to a colander to drain and cool. (Keep in mind that the vegetables, and even different parts of the same vegetable, may require different cooking times.)

Drain the soaking liquid from the salt cod. Bring a heavy saucepan of water to a boil and add the cod. Cook, stirring occasionally, until it is medium-rare, about 5 minutes. Drain, then rinse under cool running water and pat dry. Using your hands, tear the cod into medium-size pieces, discarding any cartilage, skin, and bones. In a large bowl, toss together the cod, yautia, sweet potatoes, bananas, onion, tomatoes, and oil. Spread the salad greens on a serving platter, top with the codfish and vegetable mixture, and distribute the avocados and egg slices on top. Serve immediately or cover and chill in the refrigerator until ready to serve. If serving cold, add the green banana and avocado just before serving so they don't turn brown.

There is always a gratin on the menu at Santaella. Sometimes it's a classic recipe from the French tradition, but I also love experimenting with how island ingredients can find their place in this comforting preparation, so often it's a more unusual version. The inspiration for this dish comes from shepherd's pie. *Pastelón* is traditionally made up of layers of meat and potatoes, but this one is elevated with the addition of sofrito, heavy cream, and pulled pork shoulder. This recipe makes more pork shoulder than needed for the gratin. Cover and refrigerate the extra meat to use in sandwiches or soups or, as we do, heat it up and serve with rice and pigeon peas. The pork will need to marinate for at least 6 hours, so be sure to start the recipe well in advance of serving.

PASTELÓN DE LECHÓN Y BATATA CON QUESO DE BOLA
Pork and Sweet Potato Gratin

SERVES 4 TO 6

- 8 cloves garlic, peeled
- 1 tablespoon dried oregano
- 4 tablespoons kosher salt, plus more as needed
- 1 tablespoon freshly ground black pepper, plus more as needed
- 2 large fresh culantro leaves
- 3 tablespoons fresh bitter orange juice, or 1½ tablespoons each regular orange juice and lime juice
- ¼ cup extra-virgin olive oil (preferable Spanish)
- 1 (6- to 8-pound) bone-in pork shoulder
- 4 cups sofrito (page 40)
- 1 cup heavy cream
- 2 pounds yellow or orange batatas (see page 27) or sweet potatoes, peeled and cut into 2-inch chunks
- 8 tablespoons (1 stick) unsalted butter
- ½ tablespoon freshly ground nutmeg
- ½ cup shredded Edam cheese
- ½ cup shredded mozzarella cheese
- ½ cup grated Parmesan cheese

In a *pilón* (mortar and pestle), mash together the garlic, oregano, salt, pepper, and culantro until it forms a paste. Add the bitter orange juice and oil and mix well.

Put the pork shoulder in a roasting pan. Using a sharp knife, make a few incisions, about ½ inch deep, in the surface of the pork shoulder. Rub the garlic paste all over the pork shoulder, making sure to get some into the incisions. Cover and let the pork marinate in the refrigerator for 6 to 8 hours or up to overnight.

Preheat the oven to 350°F. Roast the pork for 3½ to 4 hours. Remove the pan from the oven and let the pork cool to room temperature (leave the oven on). Cut 2 pounds of the meat into ½-inch pieces and place them in a medium saucepan. (Reserve the remaining pork for another use.) Add the sofrito and cream and cook over medium heat, stirring occasionally, for 15 minutes. Taste and adjust the seasoning with salt and pepper.

Bring a medium saucepan of water to a boil. Add the sweet potato and cook until tender, about 30 minutes. Drain the sweet potatoes and return them to the saucepan. While the potatoes are still warm, add the butter and nutmeg and mash them well. Season with salt and pepper.

Spread the pork mixture evenly over the bottom of an 11-by-7-inch baking dish. Spoon the mashed sweet potato on top of the pork and spread it out evenly. Cover the top of the pastelón with the cheeses. Bake for 20 to 25 minutes, until the cheese is golden and bubbling. Serve hot.

Finding a butcher who will cut pork chops with the skin on is totally worth the effort for the reaction you'll get from your guests. Ask your butcher to cut the chops 1 inch thick and leave the fat and skin layer, as well as the rib cross section, on each (see photo). Before you fry the chops, score the outside skin and fat. We call them "cancan" chops because the frilled, glistening, crisp fat that lines the outer edge of the chop after frying looks like the skirt of a cancan girl.

CHULETAS CANCAN CON BATATA ASADA
Cancan Pork Chops with Baked Sweet Potatoes

SERVES 4

4 (¾-pound) pork chops with skin on (each 1 inch thick)
4 teaspoons kosher salt
⅛ teaspoon freshly ground black pepper
⅛ teaspoon chopped fresh oregano
2 teaspoons chopped garlic
3 cups olive oil
Batata Asada (recipe follows)

Score the skin and fat (but don't cut into the meat) of each pork chop at 1½-inch intervals, all along the edge of the chop. In a small bowl, mix together the salt, pepper, oregano, and garlic and rub the mixture all over the chops. Place the chops on a plate or tray and cover. Let sit at room temperature for about 30 minutes.

In a large, heavy skillet, heat the oil over medium-high heat. Fry the pork chops, turning them every 5 minutes, until they are deep brown and the skin is crisp, about 20 minutes total. Transfer to a paper towel-lined plate to drain briefly, then serve with the baked sweet potatoes alongside.

BATATA ASADA / BAKED SWEET POTATOES

SERVES 4

4 medium batatas (see page 27) or sweet potatoes, unpeeled
½ teaspoon kosher salt

Preheat the oven to 400°F. Line a rimmed baking sheet with aluminum foil.

Wash the sweet potatoes and pierce each one a few times with a fork. Place on the lined baking sheet and bake until tender, 45 minutes to 1 hour. Make a cut in the top of each sweet potato and season with the salt. Serve hot.

A GATHERING
AT THE COUNTRY HOUSE

—

MENU

—

ALMOJÁBANAS
Rice Flour Fritters, page 32

QUIMBOMBÓ REBOZADO SERVIDO CON CREMA DE ANCHOAS
Fried Okra with Anchovy Cream Sauce, page 57

FRICASE DE CABRITO AL CURRY CON ARROZ CÍTRICO
Curried Goat Stew with Orange and Lime Rice, page 27

ARAÑITAS
Shredded Green Plantain Fritters, page 128

BUÑUELOS DE VIENTO EN ALMÍBAR DE MANDARINA Y ANÍS
Light-as-Air Fritters in Tangerine and Anise Syrup, page 183

CHAMPAGNE

Goats are raised in the central Puerto Rican countryside where the elevation is higher and there are fields of lush vegetation for the voracious animals to munch on. Goat meat is a very common ingredient here, and cooking it fricassee style, with the bones in, makes for a supremely flavorful dish. Curry goes very well with the slightly gamey goat meat and gives a nod not only to India and Southeast Asia but also to the Caribbean people who have lovingly adopted the spice mixture.

FRICASE DE CABRITO AL CURRY CON ARROZ CÍTRICO
Curried Goat Stew with Orange and Lime Rice

SERVES 10

20 pounds bone-in goat meat, cut into 2-inch chunks
2 tablespoons kosher salt
1 tablespoon freshly ground black pepper
½ cup peanut oil
4 tablespoons red curry paste
2 tablespoons green curry paste
¼ cup Santaella curry powder (recipe follows)
5 cups diced yellow onions
2 cups canned tomato paste
1 (750-ml) bottle Cabernet Sauvignon wine
1 head garlic, cloves peeled and mashed to a paste in a mortar
5 large carrots, peeled and chopped
4 cups coconut milk, canned or fresh (page 187)
4 cups beef broth
  Arroz Blanco (page 132)
2 tablespoons extra-virgin olive oil
2 limes
1 lemon

Season the goat with the salt and pepper. In a large pot, heat the oil over high heat. Add the goat meat and sear, stirring continuously, until browned on all sides. Add the red and green curry pastes and the curry powder and sauté for 1 minute. Stir in the onions, tomato paste, wine, garlic, carrots, coconut milk, and broth. Reduce the heat to medium, cover, and cook for 1½ hours, or until the meat is tender. Uncover, stir for 30 seconds, then reduce the heat to low and cook uncovered to allow the mixture to thicken, about 20 minutes more.

To make the arroz cítrico, remove the zest from the lemon and lime. Finely chop the zests. Squeeze 1 teaspoon of juice each from a lemon and a lime. Mix the zests, juices, and olive oil into the rice while it is still hot. Serve alongside the stew.

SANTAELLA CURRY POWDER

MAKES ABOUT ½ CUP

2 tablespoons freshly ground fennel seeds
2 tablespoons freshly ground cinnamon
1 tablespoon freshly ground cumin
1 tablespoon freshly ground yellow mustard seeds
1 tablespoon freshly ground coriander seeds
1 tablespoon ground turmeric
1 tablespoon freshly ground cardamom

Mix all of the ingredients thoroughly in a bowl and store in an airtight container in a cool, dry place.

Arañitas literally translates to "little spiders" because the fried plantain shreds look like spindly-legged arachnids. As you can imagine, kids love these treats: deep-fried, plus salt, plus—did I mention they look like spiders? Fun!

Green plantains are also used to make the very well-known flattened and fried tostones, but using them in shredded form changes the whole experience—more plantain surface area being fried to a richly browned crispness makes them like a completely different vegetable.

ARAÑITAS
Shredded Green Plantain Fritters

MAKES 4 SERVINGS

2   green plantains, peeled
    Vegetable oil, for deep-frying
    Kosher salt

Grate the plantains on the large holes of a box grater. (Each plantain will yield enough for about 5 fritters.)

In a deep, heavy skillet, heat 3 inches of oil over medium-high heat to 350°F. Line a plate with paper towels.

Grab a small clump (about ¼ cup) of the grated plantain and press gently with your fingers so it will stick together a bit. Do not compress it into a ball; you want an irregular spiderlike shape.

Carefully drop the plantain bunch into the hot oil. Repeat with 3 more bunches, or as many as your skillet will hold comfortably in one layer. Fry until crisp and golden, about 7 minutes, gently turning or bobbing the fritter into the oil to ensure uniform crispness. Using tongs, carefully transfer to the paper towel–lined plate to drain and sprinkle with salt to taste. Repeat with the remaining shredded plantain and serve immediately.

Funche is a creamy cornmeal that is similar to the polenta of northern Italy and the grits of the American South, an old-fashioned country dish that's delicious and inexpensive. *Funche* acts as a subtle, creamy base that complements whatever flavors it's paired with. Traditionally, people in the Puerto Rican countryside would eat this with codfish or beans, but the veal in this recipe makes a humble dish more luxurious. The veal needs to marinate overnight in the refrigerator, so prepare this well in advance of serving.

TERNERA GUISADA SOBRE FUNCHE DE MAÍZ
Veal Stew over Puerto Rican Polenta

SERVES 4 TO 6

2   pounds veal shoulder, trimmed and cut into cubes
1   teaspoon kosher salt, plus more as needed
2   tablespoons dried oregano
6   tablespoons olive oil
4   cloves garlic, mashed to a paste in a mortar
2   cups good-quality red wine
1   onion, diced
1   cup sofrito (page 40)
1   cup tomato paste
2   carrots, peeled and diced
4   bay leaves
4   fresh culantro leaves
    Freshly ground black pepper
    Funche de maíz (recipe follows)

In a large bowl, combine the veal, salt, oregano, 4 tablespoons of the oil, the garlic, and the wine. Mix well, cover, and marinate in the refrigerator overnight.

In a heavy saucepan, heat the remaining 2 tablespoons oil over medium-high heat; add the onion and sauté until translucent, 4 to 6 minutes. Add the sofrito and sauté for 2 minutes. Add the veal with its marinade, stir well, and cook for 5 minutes. Add the tomato paste, carrots, bay leaves, culantro, and 2 cups water and reduce the heat to medium-low. Cover and cook, stirring occasionally, until the meat is tender and the sauce has thickened, about 1½ hours. Adjust the seasoning with salt and pepper to taste. Serve with the funche de maíz.

NOTE: You may use any cut of veal in this recipe, with or without bones.

FUNCHE DE MAÍZ / PUERTO RICAN POLENTA

SERVES 4 TO 6

3   cups milk
1   tablespoon butter
1   teaspoon kosher salt
½   teaspoon granulated sugar
1¼ cups yellow cornmeal

In a heavy saucepan, combine the milk, butter, salt, and sugar and bring to a boil. Whisk in the cornmeal, reduce the heat to low, and cook, stirring often, until the mixture is thick yet creamy, 10 to 12 minutes. Serve immediately.

Criollo is a term that refers to the "Puerto Ricanness" of something. For us, it means "of this place," and while there are so many dishes on the island that qualify as *criollo,* this one may be the most quintessentially Puerto Rican. Completely comforting, it is made very often at home but also easy to find in restaurants all over the island. Traditionally the dish is made with a lesser cut of meat that's pounded, tenderized with vinegar, and sautéed in olive oil, but here I use lean, buttery tenderloin and just a hint of vinegar. It's always served with white rice and pink beans.

This recipe calls for more rice and beans than you will need to serve two people, but we like to keep these things cooked so that they are always ready for mealtime, to make *arroz mamposteao* (page 135) or a late-night snack.

"BISTEC" ENCEBOLLADO CON ARROZ BLANCO Y HABICHUELAS ROSADAS
Beef Tenderloin Medallions and Sautéed Onions with Rice and Pink Beans

---

SERVES 2

8   ounces beef tenderloin
1   clove garlic, mashed to a paste in a mortar
½   teaspoon dried oregano
½   teaspoon apple cider vinegar
     Kosher salt
¾   cup extra-virgin olive oil
½   of a large white onion, sliced into thin rings
     Arroz Blanco (recipe follows), for serving
     Habichuelas Rosadas (recipe follows on page 135), for serving

From the beef tenderloin cut 2 medallions, making each about 4 ounces. With a mallet, pound each piece of meat to about ½ inch thick. Season the beef with the garlic, oregano, vinegar, and salt to taste.

In a sauté pan, heat the oil over high heat. Add the beef and sauté until it has a nice, seared, brown surface, 1 to 2 minutes on each side. Transfer the beef to a serving plate and add the onion to the sauté pan. Cook until the onion softens a bit and some brown color begins to form, about 2 minutes.

Spoon the onion over the beef and serve with the rice and beans.

ARROZ BLANCO / WHITE RICE

SERVES 4 TO 6

¼   cup extra-virgin olive oil
2   teaspoons kosher salt
2   cups short- or medium-grain white rice

In a medium saucepan, bring 3 cups water to a boil with the oil and salt. Add the rice and stir. Reduce the heat to medium, stir, and cook uncovered for 10 to 15 minutes, then stir again. Reduce the heat to low, cover the pot, and cook for 10 to 15 minutes more, until the rice is tender and all the water has been absorbed. Serve hot.

Sit down at almost any meal in a Puerto Rican household and you will very likely see a serving dish of rice and pink beans (similar to pinto or kidney beans) on the table. They are a standard side dish here, to the point of being obligatory. Needless to say, there ends up being some leftover, and this recipe is a nice way to use what isn't eaten.

ARROZ MAMPOSTEAO
Mixed Rice

SERVES 2

3   tablespoons extra-virgin olive oil
1   cup cooked Arroz Blanco (page 132)
1   cup cooked Habichuelas Rosadas (recipe below)
1   tablespoon chopped fresh cilantro
3   fresh culantro leaves

In a medium nonstick skillet, heat the oil over medium heat. Add the rice and beans, stir to combine, and cook until heated through, 3 to 4 minutes. Add the cilantro and culantro and stir to combine. Serve hot.

HABICHUELAS ROSADAS / PINK BEANS

SERVES 4 TO 6

Make sure to allow enough time for soaking the beans overnight. If you can't find pink beans you can substitute light red kidney beans. "Caribbean pumpkin" refers to *calabaza,* but you can substitute any eating pumpkin (sweet or pie pumpkin) or a butternut squash.

1   pound dried pink beans, soaked in water to cover overnight, drained
½   pound bone-in smoked ham
1   tablespoon annatto oil (page 40)
2   tablespoons extra-virgin olive oil
1½   cups sofrito (page 40)
1   tablespoon dried oregano
½   cup tomato paste
1   cup diced calabaza Caribbean pumpkin (see page 27; peeled or unpeeled, seeded)
¼   cup chopped fresh culantro
3   sprigs fresh cilantro
        Kosher salt and freshly ground black pepper
        Arroz Blanco (page 132), for serving

In a large, heavy pot, pour enough water to cover the beans and the ham by 2 inches. Bring to a boil over medium-high heat, then reduce the heat to medium-low. Simmer the beans until tender, about 45 minutes. Drain them in a colander set over a pot, reserving the cooking water. Carefully remove the meat from the ham bone and add to the beans. Discard the bone.

In a saucepan, combine the annatto oil, olive oil, and sofrito. Sauté over medium-high heat for 2 to 3 minutes. Add the oregano and tomato paste and cook for 1 minute more. Add the beans and the pumpkin. Using a ladle, add 2 cups of the reserved bean cooking liquid and cook until the pumpkin is tender and the mixture is thick, about 30 minutes, adding more cooking liquid as needed. Add the culantro and cilantro and stir well. Taste and adjust the seasoning. Serve hot over white rice.

RICE AND *PEGAO*

So many Latin and Caribbean cultures rely on rice, not only to fill space on the plate with other dishes but as an important and integral ingredient in recipes.

Puerto Rico is no exception, and we take pride in being expert rice cooks—plain rice is perhaps the first dish a child might learn to cook, and Puerto Ricans take their technique very seriously. Short-grain rice and medium-grain, Spanish-style white rice are the two typically used in Puerto Rico. Medium-grain rice is able to absorb lots of water yet still retain its shape, producing a fluffy, slightly dry rice; short-grain rice retains a little bit of stickiness. While it may seem simple, cooking a perfect pot of rice does take practice. Seasoned cooks are very loyal to the brand of rice they use as well as to the pot, or *caldero*, they use to cook the rice. Each cook must find his or her own method, and I encourage you to keep working to determine which techniques work best for you.

The rice, the pot, the method and the finishing are all crucial to achieving rice with a good texture and the cherished *pegao,* the crunchy, browned rice that sticks to the bottom of the *caldero*. What many may think is a mistake, Puerto Ricans treasure as the best part of the rice. The formula for our style of rice is generally two parts water to one part uncooked rice. Stir in about ¼ cup vegetable oil and a little salt. The traditional *caldero* is essential, because the shape of the vessel allows the water to evaporate evenly and the cast-aluminum surface conducts heat very well and evenly. *Pegao* is achieved by cooking the rice to perfect tenderness and raising the heat in the last five to ten minutes of cooking to encourage a little browning on the bottom (see recipe on page 132). When serving the rice, it is customary to scoop mostly properly cooked white rice onto the plate and then top it with a little bit of the *pegao*—but don't take it all! To take more than just a couple bites' worth of *pegao* would be considered rude.

On the northern part of the island, the area known as Guánica is home to one of the better fishing harbors in Puerto Rico. I love visiting so I can meet the fishermen and buy from them directly (the nearby seafood restaurants are also not to be missed). Almost always available: conch, queen snapper, and grouper.

I love a dramatic presentation. When a whole fish, cooked perfectly and dressed with bright herbs and vegetables, hits the table, people really respond. Red snapper is a perfect fish for frying whole. The result is super-crisp skin and—my favorite part—a crisp-crunchy tail. The tomato and pineapple dressing that is served with it acts as a salsa and supplies a fresh, acidic accompaniment to both the fish and the fried plantains.

CHILLO ENTERO FRITO EN ADEREZO DE CILANTRO, TOMATE Y PIÑA

Fried Whole Red Snapper with Tomato, Pineapple, and Cilantro Dressing

SERVES 2

1   whole red snapper
    (1 to 1½ pounds), cleaned
    Kosher salt
4   cloves garlic, mashed to a paste
    in a mortar
1½ cups all-purpose flour
    Vegetable oil, for deep-frying
    Tomato and Pineapple Sauce
    (recipe follows), for serving
1   lime, cut into wedges (optional)
    Tostones (page 166), for serving
    Cilantro leaves, for garnish

Using a sharp knife, make a few small hash marks on the surface of the fish. This will keep it from curling up too much when fried. Season both sides of the fish with salt and the garlic. Put the flour on a large plate or tray and dredge the fish in the flour, shaking off any excess.

Fill a deep-fryer according to the manufacturer's directions or fill a large, heavy pot with about 5 inches of oil. Heat the oil to about 350°F. Line a tray with paper towels.

Fry the whole fish until golden and crisp, about 10 minutes. Transfer the fish to the paper towel–lined tray to drain briefly.

Serve hot, with a little of the tomato and pineapple sauce poured over the top and the rest on the side, along with the lime if you like, and tostones. Garnish with some cilantro leaves.

TOMATO AND PINEAPPLE DRESSING

MAKES 1 CUP

¼   cup chopped fresh cilantro
    Juice of 1 lime
½   tablespoon apple cider vinegar
½   clove garlic, mashed to a paste in a mortar
1   teaspoon kosher salt
½   teaspoon freshly ground black pepper
1   cup olive oil
1   tomato, finely diced
½   cup diced fresh pineapple

Put the cilantro, lime juice, vinegar, garlic, salt, and pepper in a blender and blend for about 1 minute. With the blender running on low speed, slowly pour in the oil.

Pour the mixture into a small bowl, add the tomato and pineapple, and gently stir to combine.

PLÁTANOS

Besides their delicious taste, it's the versatility of *plátanos* that blows my mind.

Beyond the very familiar *tostones*, the fried green plantains that so many people know (and that all of us love), Puerto Rican cuisine offers recipes utilizing them in every form—smashed, grated, fried, roasted, grilled, pickled, boiled, you name it. Originating in Africa, plantains were traded in Old World Europe by the Portuguese and made their way to the New World on Spanish exploration ships. The tropical plant was at home in the Caribbean and became a popular crop in all of the islands as well as Central and South America. Plantains are related to bananas, and grow in the same way. The trees produce large bunches of "hands" (similar to a single bunch of bananas) from large flower pods that grow on stalks. When the plantains reach the point where they are mature in size but still bright green in color, the stalks are harvested and taken to markets. Shopping at one of the markets in Puerto Rico or in an international market, you will no doubt see gorgeous displays boasting the large bunches of green plantains still on the stalk. You will also find plantains that are yellow and reddish—turning toward black. The green *(verde)* is firm and quite starchy and at this point a bit more like a starchy tuber in texture than a fruit. The green plantains can hold up against vigorous preparation methods like grating, mashing, frying, and boiling. Yellow plantains *(pintón)* are turning from green to yellow and may have a few black spots on them. This stage is when the starchy flesh begins to develop more sugars and get a bit softer. They are still good for frying and boiling at this point and will provide a tiny bit more sweetness than green plantains. Ripe plantains *(amarillo)* are yellow with lots of black developing on their peels. They will be much sweeter and have only a bit of starchiness left. Now—and even when they turn completely black—they are great roasted, grilled, or sautéed in butter. Ripe plantains will caramelize nicely when fried, as in the Piñon de Amarillos (page 169).When they start turning completely black and are very soft, they are at the stage that in Spanish is called *maduro*. Some Puerto Ricans have a funny saying: Just before the flies have taken over the fruit is the point of *maduro* and when the fruit is at its sweetest. The shiny, slick leaves of the plantain tree are also utilized in our kitchens. Sold alongside the plantains in the market, they can become liners for baking pans, vehicles for steaming fish, and wraps for boiled or baked recipes such as the delicious *pasteles* on page 151. The leaves are beautiful and may also be used as table décor, lining serving trays, displayed in large vases, or even set out as serving plates for certain foods. If fresh leaves are not available in your area, look for frozen banana or plantain leaves.

Arroz con pollo is perhaps the most popular dish across all of Latin America and the Caribbean. Each family has its own way of seasoning and serving it, but it is still the same basic dish. Cooking your own version is like riffing on a classic song. What follows is how I make it at Santaella, but you should feel free to improvise. Be sure to leave time for the chicken to rest in the refrigerator overnight.

SANTAELLA ARROZ CON POLLO Y AMARILLOS FRITOS
Santaella Rice with Chicken and Fried Sweet Plaintains

SERVES 6 TO 8

- 1   (5-pound) chicken, cut into serving pieces
- 2   tablespoons adobo seasoning (page 144)
- 2   red bell peppers
- ½   cup olive oil
- ⅓   cup annatto oil (page 40)
- 2   cups sofrito (page 40)
- ½   cup tomato paste
- 2   cups alcaparrado (page 41)
- 1¼ cups beer (any lighter-style beer will do)
- 3   cups medium-grain white rice
- 3½ cups chicken stock
- ½   cup extra-virgin olive oil
     Kosher salt and freshly ground black pepper
     Fried Sweet Plantains (page 144), for serving

Rub the chicken pieces with the adobo seasoning, place them in a baking dish, cover, and let them rest in the refrigerator overnight.

Roast the bell peppers by putting them in direct contact with the flame on your stove, turning them with tongs until most of the skin is blistered and black. (You can also roast them under the broiler in your oven; watch them closely and turn them often to achieve the same black, blistered skin.) When the peppers are still hot, place them in a paper bag and seal. The steam will make the blistered skin easy to rub off. When the peppers are cool enough to handle, peel off the black skin (some small bits may remain), cut out the core and seeds, and slice the flesh into 1-inch pieces. Set aside.

In a large *caldero* (or in a Dutch oven or saucepan), heat the olive oil and annatto oil over high heat. Add the chicken pieces and sauté, turning often so that the chicken begins to brown on all sides, about 5 minutes. Transfer the chicken to a platter and pour the excess oil from the pot. In the same pot, sauté the sofrito, tomato paste, and alcaparrado together over medium-high heat for about 3 minutes. Return the chicken pieces to the pot and pour in the beer. Reduce the heat to medium and cook for 5 minutes. Stir in the rice.

Meanwhile, in a small saucepan, bring the stock to a boil. Pour the boiling chicken stock into the pot with the chicken and rice. Return to a boil and then reduce the heat to low. When there is only a small amount of liquid left in the pot, cover and continue simmering until the rice is cooked through, about 30 minutes.

Remove from the heat and stir in the extra-virgin olive oil and the roasted red peppers. Season to taste with salt and pepper and serve with the fried sweet plantains.

AMARILLOS FRITOS / FRIED SWEET PLANTAINS

It's up to you how to slice sweet plantains for frying. I prefer to cut them lengthwise into ¼-inch planks because their thinness leads to more surface area, which means more caramelization. But others like to cut them into ½-inch slices on the bias; some find these smaller pieces easier to manage in the skillet.

SERVES 6 TO 8

3   ripe yellow plantains, peeled and sliced
    Corn oil, for shallow-frying

In a large skillet, heat about ½ inch of oil set over medium-high heat until shimmering, about 350°F. Fry the plantain slices until caramelized, about 2 minutes on each side. Serve hot.

ADOBO SEASONING

Adobo is a general term for a rub or paste that is used to marinate an ingredient to prepare it for cooking. Different Spanish-influenced countries use the word to refer to many varieties of the mixture, and of course each cook usually has his own special recipe. In my recipes, when I refer to "adobo" I am using this simple dry spice mix that I keep on hand at all times. It's so easy, there is no reason to ever buy store-bought adobo again.

MAKES ½ CUP

2   tablespoons dried oregano
2   tablespoons onion powder
2   tablespoons garlic powder
1   tablespoon kosher salt
1   tablespoon freshly ground black pepper

Combine all the ingredients together and mix well. Store in an airtight container for up to 3 months.

Simmering a main ingredient with onions, garlic, tomatoes, peppers, and herbs is a technique that's ubiquitous in Puerto Rico. The flavors of each element are coaxed out with a preliminary sauté in plenty of olive oil, then a longer, gentler simmer. Eggplant, which thrives in very hot weather, is abundant on the island, and its meaty texture holds up well to the stewing process. I like to serve this as a side dish, but it makes a wonderful vegetarian entrée as well.

BERENJENAS GUISADAS
Eggplant Stew

SERVES 4

- ½   cup extra-virgin olive oil
- 1   large yellow onion, finely chopped
- 5   cloves garlic, mashed to a paste in a mortar
- 2 to 3 eggplants (about 2½ pounds), peeled and cut into ½-inch cubes
- 1   cubanelle pepper, finely diced
- ¾   cup diced fresh tomato
- 1   tablespoon tomato paste
- ½   teaspoon ground cumin
- ½   tablespoon dried oregano
- 1   tablespoon capers
- 2   tablespoons chopped fresh cilantro

In a nonstick skillet, heat the oil over medium-high heat. Add the onion and garlic and sauté for 2 minutes. Stir in the eggplant and cook for 2 minutes more. Reduce the heat to medium, add the cubanelle pepper, diced tomato, tomato paste, cumin, oregano, and capers, and cook, stirring occasionally, for 15 minutes or until the eggplant has achieved a velvety texture. Remove from the heat, add the cilantro, and mix well. Serve hot.

There is no doubt that *mofongo* is the most famous Puerto Rican recipe—well, perhaps with the exception of the piña colada. Green plantains are fried and then mashed with crisp pork cracklings and garlic. The mashing, preferably in a *pilón,* or mortar and pestle, is important to create the correct texture, and the action draws out the flavors and marries them completely. At its most basic, the mash is delicious and filling. When elevated with fillings like this rock lobster (also called spiny lobster) and a white wine sauce, it becomes rich and elegant.

MOFONGO RELLENO DE LANGOSTA EN CREMA CRIOLLA DE VINO BLANCO
Mashed Plantains Stuffed with Rock Lobster in Creole Wine Sauce

SERVES 4

FOR THE MOFONGO:

Vegetable oil, for deep-frying

4 green plantains, peeled and cut into 1-inch chunks

4 cloves garlic

1 teaspoon kosher salt

1 cup chicharrón or crisp cooked bacon

¼ cup good-quality olive oil

FOR THE LOBSTER FILLING:

1 yellow onion, diced

2 cloves garlic, mashed to a paste in a mortar

¼ tablespoon dried oregano

1 cubanero pepper, diced

½ tablespoon tomato paste

1 tablespoon olive oil

¾ cup white wine

½ cup heavy cream

2 fresh Caribbean lobster tails, cut into 1-inch pieces

Kosher salt

2 tablespoons chopped fresh cilantro

MAKE THE MOFONGO: In a heavy skillet, heat 3 inches of vegetable oil over medium-high heat to about 350°F. Line a plate with paper towels.

Fry the plantains in the hot oil until they start to turn golden, about 5 minutes. Using a slotted spoon, transfer the plantains to the paper towel–lined plate to drain. (This is the same as the first step in making tostones, page 166.)

In a large *pilón* (mortar and pestle), mash 1 of the garlic cloves until very mushy. Add one-quarter of the plantain chunks and ¼ teaspoon of the salt and continue mashing. Add ¼ cup of the cracklings, drizzle in a little of the olive oil to add moisture, and keep mashing until it is all very well combined and has formed a doughlike paste. Press the pestle into the center of the mixture to form a hollow. Use a spoon to loosen the edges, then flip the mofongo out onto a plate. Flip the mofongo once again onto a serving plate so that the hollow cup faces up. This is where your lobster filling will go. Repeat to create three more mofongo cups. (Alternatively, you can form the mofongo into balls and use the pestle to create a well in each on the serving plates.)

MAKE THE LOBSTER FILLING: In a large skillet, sauté the onion, garlic, oregano, and cubanero pepper over medium-high heat until the onion is soft and translucent, about 5 minutes. Reduce the heat to medium and add the tomato paste and cook, stirring continuously, for 2 minutes. Raise the heat to high and add the wine and cream. Let the mixture reduce until thickened a bit, about 5 minutes. Stir in the lobster pieces and cook for 3 minutes more. Remove from the heat, season with salt, and sprinkle in the cilantro.

Spoon the hot lobster mixture into the mofongo cups and serve immediately.

Queen snapper is a type of red snapper but from deeper waters. This white, firm-fleshed fish is one of my favorites: It's very flavorful and goes wonderfully with this elegant sauce made from acerolas. Acerolas are also called Caribbean cherries and grow throughout the islands, South and Central America, and in some parts of Florida and Texas. A breadfruit puree completes the trio of favorite ingredients of Puerto Rico.

The acerola juice can be made up to three days ahead of time and kept in the refrigerator. If you can't find acerola fruit or juice you can use equal parts fresh cranberries and cherries.

FILETE DE CARTUCHO ASADO EN SALSA DE ACEROLA SOBRE PURE DE PANA

Roasted Queen Snapper in Caribbean Cherry and Butter Sauce over Breadfruit Puree

SERVES 6

FOR THE FRESH ACEROLA JUICE:
1½ cups fresh ripe acerolas
2 tablespoons granulated sugar
1½ tablespoons good-quality balsamic vinegar

FOR THE BREADFRUIT PUREE:
1 (3- to 4-pound) breadfruit (see page 27)
1 tablespoon kosher salt, plus more as needed
4 tablespoons (½ stick) butter
3 tablespoons olive oil
Pinch of freshly grated nutmeg

FOR THE FISH:
6 (6- to 8-ounce) skin-on queen snapper (cartucho) fillets
6 tablespoons olive oil
Kosher salt

FOR THE ACEROLA BUTTER SAUCE:
¼ cup good-quality Puerto Rican light rum
¼ cup apple cider vinegar
2 tablespoons finely chopped shallot
⅓ cup heavy cream
¼ teaspoon kosher salt, or more to taste
⅛ teaspoon ground white pepper, or more to taste
1 cup (2 sticks) butter, cut into tablespoon-size pieces and chilled

MAKE THE FRESH ACEROLA JUICE: In a bowl, crush the acerolas with a mortar, then add the sugar and vinegar and mix well. Set aside to macerate for 2 hours at room temperature, or cover and refrigerate up to overnight. Add ¾ cup water, stir well, and pass the mixture through a fine-mesh sieve set over a bowl, pressing down until all the liquid has been extracted. Discard the solids. You'll need 1 cup of the acerola juice, at room temperature, for the sauce; keep any leftover juice in an airtight container in the refrigerator for another use.

MAKE THE BREADFRUIT PUREE: Peel the breadfruit and cut it into 1-inch cubes. Put the breadfruit in a medium saucepan and add water to cover by at least 1 inch. Add the salt, bring to a boil over medium-high heat, and cook until tender, 8 to 10 minutes. Drain the breadfruit, return to the pan, and mash with the butter, oil, and nutmeg. Add salt to taste and keep warm.

MAKE THE FISH: Preheat the oven to 350°F. Lightly oil a baking sheet.

Cut two or three 1-inch-long incisions in the skin of each fillet. This will keep the fillet from curling up when cooked. Rub the fillets with the oil, sprinkle with salt, and place skin side up on the prepared baking sheet. Bake for 8 to 10 minutes, until cooked all the way through.

MEANWHILE, MAKE THE ACEROLA SAUCE: In a heavy saucepan, combine the rum, vinegar, and shallot and cook over medium-high heat for about 5 minutes, until reduced by half. Add the cream, salt, and white pepper and bring to a boil. Cook for 1 minute, stirring if necessary. Reduce the heat to low and add a few tablespoons of the butter, whisking continuously. While whisking, add the remaining butter a few pieces at a time—adding each piece before the previous pieces have melted completely and lifting the pan from the heat occasionally to cool the mixture. Remove from the heat, season to taste with salt and white pepper, then pour the sauce through a fine-mesh sieve into a saucepan, pressing on the shallots to push all of the sauce through. Whisk in the reserved 1 cup acerola juice. Taste and adjust the seasoning.

Spoon some of the breadfruit puree in the middle of each plate, top each serving with one fish fillet, and pour some of the the acerola butter sauce over the fish. Serve immediately.

Of the many different recipes in Puerto Rico that are traditionally served around Christmas and rarely at other times of the year, I'd say that the most famous are *pasteles*. These are a bit like tamales, but made with yautia instead of corn. The "dough," for lack of a better word, is spooned into a square cut from a banana leaf. Savory fillings are encased in the dough, the whole thing is wrapped in the leaf like a little package and tied with string, and the packages are cooked in simmering water. They do take time to make, but during the holidays, when friends and family are gathered, the all-day task is shared—along with lots of laughs and probably some singing. Start these a day in advance, as the yautia mixture needs to rest in the refrigerator overnight.

PASTELES DE MASA CON CERDO SERVIDO CON ARROZ CON GANDULES
Steamed Pork Dumplings with Rice and Pigeon Peas

MAKES 14 TO 16 PASTELES

FOR THE YAUTIA DOUGH:
2½ pounds yautia (see page 27), peeled
3 pounds green bananas, peeled
¼ cup annatto oil (page 40)
1 teaspoon kosher salt

FOR THE PORK FILLING:
¼ cup olive oil
½ pound pork loin or boneless pork shoulder, finely diced
1 tablespoon kosher salt
5 ounces smoked ham, diced
1 cup sofrito (page 40)
½ cup tomato paste
¼ cup raisins
¼ cup canned chickpeas
½ cup pitted green olives, sliced
1 tablespoon dried oregano
1 red bell pepper, roasted, peeled, seeded and sliced into strips (see page 157)

FOR COOKING AND SERVING:
Annatto oil (page 40)
16 (8-by-10-inch) pieces plantain or banana leaves (thawed, if frozen)
Rice with Pigeon Peas (page 152)

MAKE THE YAUTIA DOUGH: Grate the yautia and green bananas on the small holes of a box grater into a bowl. Pour in the annatto oil, season with the salt, and mix gently to form a dough. Cover and refrigerate overnight.

MAKE THE PORK FILLING: In a large skillet, heat the oil over medium heat. Season the pork evenly with the salt and add it to the skillet along with the ham. Sauté, stirring occasionally, for about 5 minutes. Reduce the heat to medium-low and add the sofrito, tomato paste, raisins, chickpeas, olives, and oregano. Cook, stirring occasionally, for about 20 minutes. Remove from the heat and let cool for 30 minutes.

ASSEMBLE THE PASTELES: Bring a large pot of water to a boil. Place a sheet of parchment paper on your work surface. One at a time, heat a plantain leaf over an open flame for a couple of seconds, moving it all around to warm the leaf to make it more flexible for wrapping. Set the leaf on the parchment-covered work surface and brush the entire surface of the leaf with annatto oil.

Spread ½ cup of the yautia dough in the center of the leaf, place 2 to 3 tablespoons of the pork filling in the center of the dough, and top with 2 or 3 roasted pepper strips. Place 2 more tablespoons of the dough on top to cover the filling. You should have a rectangle about 3½ inches wide and 6 inches long. Fold in the edges of the plantain leaf along with the parchment paper to make a square package. Tie like a parcel with butcher's twine. Repeat with more parchment paper and the remaining plantain leaves, dough, and filling.

Add the pasteles to the boiling water and cook for about 45 minutes, turning the pasteles at least once. Remove from the water. Unwrap the pasteles, removing both the parchment paper and the plantain leaf, and serve with the rice with pigeon peas.

ARROZ CON GANDULES / RICE WITH PIGEON PEAS

SERVES 6 TO 8

White rice, cooked so a little bit of crust *(pegao)* forms in the bottom of the pan, is served with almost every meal in the Puerto Rican home. Pigeon peas are so prevalent on the island and such a common ingredient that they too end up on the table as a side dish. Serving the two together is for a Puerto Rican what black beans and rice would be to a Cuban or pinto beans and rice is in parts of Mexico. Pigeon peas are smaller and don't need as much cooking time as those larger legumes, and they have a nice, green, fresh flavor.

1   tablespoon olive oil
½   cup sofrito (page 40)
½   cup (4 ounces) chopped cooked ham
2   cups medium-grain white rice
1   tablespoon dried oregano
1   (15-ounce) can pigeon peas, undrained, or 1 pound frozen or fresh pigeon peas, cooked in boiling water for 30 minutes or until tender
10   green olives, pitted and roughly chopped

In a sauté pan, heat the oil over medium-high heat. Add the sofrito and ham and sauté for about 1 minute. Pour in 4 cups water, the rice, oregano, pigeon peas, and olives and bring to a boil. Cook for about 3 minutes, then cover and reduce the heat to medium-low; cook for about 40 minutes, stirring occasionally, until the rice is tender. Serve hot.

PASTELES

The Taíno Indians of the Caribbean were resourceful and innovative when it came to food. Figuring out the nuances of various root vegetables and the best methods for cooking them was a skill that went beyond simply how to get nutrition into the body; it was the birth of our cuisine.

For instance, using a natural resource such as a large, sturdy leaf to wrap and cook food in, and setting aside certain foods for seasonal rituals has led us to one of our beloved Christmastime foods, *pasteles*. Grated root vegetables such as taro and *apio* are blended with green plantains to create a paste and then troweled onto a clean square of banana leaf. A dollop of savory vegetables, beef, fish, or pork goes in the center, and the whole affair is wrapped up in an individual-serving-sized bundle and dunked in salted boiling water. While homemade *pasteles* are becoming more rare (the process is somewhat involved and time-consuming, so restaurants and markets specializing in them do a bustling business around the holidays), making *pasteles* together as a family has long been a fun Christmastime tradition in Puerto Rico. Each step can be perfected by a different family member, assembly-line fashion. In fact, this is a great way to teach children about cooking Puerto Rican food, since the recipe features several important elements of the cuisine: making sofrito and broth, grating and mashing plantains and root vegetables, and cutting, filling, and tying banana-leaf wrappers.

Mallorca is a flaky, Spanish-style sweet bread that is available in all of the *panaderías* in Puerto Rico. It's baked in beautiful round loaves and sprinkled with confectioners' sugar. Cut into cubes and mixed with spicy, salty chorizo sausage in this stuffing for Cornish hens, the mallorca bread contributes just the right amount of sweetness. If you can't find mallorca, you can substitute any plain sweet bread such as brioche, challah, or cornbread.

GALLINITAS RELLENAS DE PAN DE MALLORCA Y CHORIZO
Cornish Hens Stuffed with Sweet Bread and Chorizo

SERVES 6

FOR THE CORNISH HENS:

2	mallorca buns (page 229), or 2 cups torn plain sweet bread
1	tablespoon butter
4	tablespoons olive oil
2	cups diced onions
1	cup diced Spanish chorizo (casing removed)
¾	cup chicken broth
2	tablespoons chopped fresh sage leave
6	cloves garlic, mashed to a paste in a mortar
	Kosher salt and freshly ground black peppers
3	Cornish hens

FOR THE PASSION FRUIT GLAZE:

	Pulp from 3 fresh passion fruits, or about 1 cup pulp, thawed if frozen
½	cup granulated sugar
1	tablespoon apple cider vinegar

MAKE THE CORNISH HENS: Tear the mallorca into bite-size pieces and place in a large bowl. In a saucepan, melt the butter with 1 tablespoon of the oil over low heat, then add the onions and cook until translucent, 3 to 4 minutes. Add the chorizo and cook for about 2 minutes, then transfer to the bowl with the bread and mix well. Pour in the broth and mix until the bread has absorbed all of the liquid. Let cool a bit, then add the sage.

Mix together the remaining 3 tablespoons oil, the garlic, and salt and pepper to taste and rub the mixture all over the hens. Stuff each hen completely with the stuffing. Place the hens in a baking dish, breast side up, and roast until cooked through and golden brown, about 45 minutes.

MEANWHILE, MAKE THE PASSION FRUIT GLAZE: In a small saucepan, combine all of the ingredients with 1 cup water, bring to a simmer over medium heat, and cook until the mixture has reduced by half, about 20 minutes. Pour through a fine-mesh sieve into a bowl, discarding the solids.

Immediately after removing the hens from the oven, pour the glaze over them and serve hot.

In the early part of 2011, Puerto Ricans opened their newspapers to find headlines using the word horror in bold type. There had been no natural disaster, no heinous crime—the declaration was reflecting the genuine feelings the island's citizens had regarding a serious shortage of canned corned beef. Introduced to the island decades ago, the salt-cured beef product packed into cans was originally essential because there is no need to refrigerate it and it has a long shelf life. Innovative cooks on the island came up with delicious recipes integrating the meat into dishes featuring plantains, all types of root vegetables, rice, and pigeon peas. Canned corned beef has become a legitimate favorite comfort food here (much as Spam has in Hawaii), with lots of home cooks utilizing it at least once a week. It's easy to see why a shortage of the beloved ingredient rocked our world for a few months.

Piononos, rolled-up plantain slices filled with meat and fried, are usually made with regular ground beef, but I like using salty corned beef because it is such a nice complement to the sweet plantains.

PIONONOS RELLENOS DE CORNED BEEF
Sweet Plantain Fritter Filled with Corned Beef

SERVES 10 TO 12

3 tablespoons olive oil
1 large yellow onion, finely diced
3 cloves garlic, mashed to a paste in a mortar
1 tablespoon annatto oil (page 40)
2 tablespoons dried oregano
1 tablespoon tomato paste
2 (11-ounce) cans corned beef
¼ cup pimento-stuffed green olives
2 tablespoons chopped fresh cilantro
Kosher salt
5 ripe sweet plantains, peeled and cut lengthwise into ¼-inch-thick slices
2 cups canola oil
3 large eggs, lightly beaten
1½ tablespoons all-purpose flour

In a skillet, heat the olive oil over medium-high heat until shimmering. Add the onion and garlic and sauté until the onion is soft, about 4 minutes. Add the annatto oil, oregano, and tomato paste and cook, stirring continuously, for 1 minute. Add the corned beef, breaking the meat apart with a wooden spoon, and cook, stirring occasionally, for 5 minutes. Stir in the olives and cilantro. Season with salt to taste, remove from the heat, and let cool.

Take one plantain slice and cup it in your hand. Place a few tablespoons of the filling in the middle of the plantain, then roll the plantain around it to form a cylinder, securing the ends with a toothpick. Set aside on a baking sheet. Repeat the process with all of the plantains and filling.

In a heavy skillet, heat the oil over medium-high heat to 350°F. Line a plate with paper towels.

While the oil is heating, in a shallow bowl, whisk together the eggs, flour, and 2 tablespoons water until completely combined. Dip each of the filled plantain rolls into the egg mixture to coat and immediately transfer to the hot oil. Fry the piononos, turning gently, until golden brown on the outside, about 3 minutes. Using a slotted spoon, transfer to the paper towel–lined plate to drain. Remove the toothpicks and serve warm.

With sofrito and *culantro* leaves as a flavor base, this comforting and restorative chicken soup is totally Puerto Rican. My father was a great cook, and he made asopao de pollo often. He garnished it at the end with a generous heap of shaved Parmesan, with roasted red peppers and sweet green peas on top. He'd make it for everyday meals, but he'd also cook up pots of it for parties at the house. Puerto Ricans love to party, and asopao de pollo is widely known as a great dish to serve to guests after a night of drinking and dancing—a delicious way to help your friends sober up before sending them on their way home.

ASOPAO DE POLLO
Chicken and Rice Soup

SERVES 6

1	cup medium-grain white rice
1	(5-pound) chicken, cut into 8 pieces
4	cups sofrito (page 40)
1	carrot, peeled and diced
3	bay leaves
5	fresh culantro leaves
1	teaspoon freshly ground black pepper, or more to taste
1	tablespoon kosher salt, or more to taste
1	cup fresh (or frozen) shelled green peas

FOR THE ROASTED RED BELL PEPPERS:

2	red bell peppers

In a large bowl, cover the rice with water and allow to soak for about 30 minutes.

In a large pot, pour 10 cups water over the chicken pieces and bring to a boil over high heat. Reduce the heat to medium. Drain the rice and add it to the chicken mixture along with the sofrito, carrot, bay leaves, culantro, black pepper, and salt and cook until the chicken and the rice are fully cooked and the liquid has thickened a bit, about 30 minutes. Taste and adjust the seasoning with salt and pepper.

Meanwhile, boil the peas for 1 minute in salted water to cover, until they are tender. Drain and set aside.

MEANWHILE, MAKE THE ROASTED RED BELL PEPPERS: Roast the bell pepper by putting it in direct contact with the flame on your stove, turning it with tongs until most of the skin is blistered and black. (You can also roast it under the broiler in your oven; watch it closely and turn it often to achieve the same black, blistered skin.) When the pepper is still hot, place it in a paper bag and seal. The steam will make the blistered skin easy to rub off. When the pepper is cool enough to handle, peel off the black skin (some small bits may remain), cut out the core and seeds, and slice the flesh into long strips. Set aside.

To serve, ladle the soup into individual bowls. Garnish with the roasted peppers and the peas.

Suckling pig is a small young pig that's the perfect size for roasting whole and serving family style. In Puerto Rico, people will order a roasted suckling pig from a restaurant or one of the roadside *lechoneras*, or barbecue stands, to take home and use in recipes or to serve along with homemade vegetable dishes and rice, but if you are lucky enough to have a source for suckling pig it's easy to make at home.

If you have leftovers, this is the pork to use in the *lechón* sandwich on page 81.

COCHINILLO ASADO CON MELAO Y RON PERFUMADO
Roast Suckling Pig with Spiced Rum and Molasses Glaze

SERVES 6 TO 8

1   (6-pound) suckling pig
    Kosher salt and freshly ground black pepper
½   cup light olive oil (preferably Spanish)
1½ cups golden rum
1   tablespoon minced shallot
½   teaspoon ground cloves
½   cup molasses
½   teaspoon chopped fresh rosemary leaves

Preheat the oven to 425°F.

Season the pig inside and out with salt and pepper. Place the pig in a large roasting pan and wrap the ears in aluminum foil to prevent them from burning. Pour the oil over the pig and place in the oven. Roast for about 2½ hours, basting often with the pan drippings. Remove the pig from the oven when it's fully cooked and let it rest for 20 to 30 minutes.

Meanwhile, in a saucepan over medium heat, bring the rum, shallot, and cloves to a simmer. Add the molasses and cook for about 5 minutes, until the mixture has a syrupy consistency. Remove from the heat and stir in the rosemary.

Using a very sharp knife, cut the pork into serving pieces. Pour the glaze over the pieces and serve immediately.

Live local land crabs are available at markets near the ocean where they feed them a "finishing diet" of corn, root vegetables, and fruit and allow them to grow. They have sweet meat similar to that of blue crabs, which you can use here if you can't find land crabs. This dish, in which crab is paired with coconut milk, a natural accompaniment, can be served in a large bowl, or, for more fun, spooned into half of a coconut shell.

ARROZ CON JUEYES AL COCO
Coconut Rice with Land Crab

SERVES 6 TO 8

5 tablespoons olive oil
2 tablespoons annatto oil (page 40)
1 cup sofrito (page 40)
½ cup tomato paste
1½ pounds local land crab or blue crabmeat, picked over and any bits of shell removed
1 tablespoon kosher salt, plus more to taste
5 cups medium-grain white rice
2 cups coconut milk (page 187)
2 tablespoons chopped fresh culantro leaves
2 tablespoons chopped fresh cilantro
    Freshly ground black pepper

In a large pot, combine the olive oil, annatto oil, sofrito, and tomato paste and cook, stirring continuously, over high heat. Add the crabmeat and salt and cook for 2 to 3 minutes. Stir in the rice, mix well, and add the coconut milk and 4 cups water. Bring to a boil, and when the liquid starts to evaporate, reduce the heat to low. Cover and cook until the rice is tender, about 20 minutes. Add the culantro and cilantro, taste and adjust the seasoning, and serve immediately.

LAND CRABS

Prehistoric and perhaps a bit creepy, *jueyes,* or land crabs, are a very common food on the island.

They are so common here that we are a bit surprised when visitors start asking so many questions about them. The crabs make their home on the soft land near the water, in holes along the shore. They start out small but become much larger than the small land crabs that most people from the States are used to seeing at water's edge, and even beefier than the typical blue crab from the southeastern coast of the States. The larger ones, some reaching the size and girth of an American football, are heavy and strong. Once caught, the crabs must be kept and fed for a few days so that they can be purged of any food that may make their meat taste too gamey. Because they are scavengers, their natural diet can make them taste a bit off, but keeping them in cages or large enclosures—feeding them on corn, coconut, bananas, and various root vegetables—cleans them out and "finishes" them in the same way a livestock producer might finish a hog with acorns or grain. The large cages that are visible on the properties of restaurants that serve them are quite a spectacle: Filled with huge numbers of crabs of various sizes, it's like looking at a strange exhibit at a museum or zoo as they scurry around making strange clicking noises when they walk. Sometimes they are aggressive—waving large, intimidating claws at viewers and other crabs. The meat is delicious, however, and some of Puerto Rico's most beloved dishes are made from these interesting creatures.

Many of the traditional foods of Puerto Rico at first glance seem beguilingly simple. What's so special about a chicken stew, for example? But dig a little deeper and you'll discover one of the many reasons I remain totally in love with the food of my homeland even as I travel around the world trying—and enjoying—new and ever more refined dishes. It has to do with the way the flavors that made their way here from Europe and Africa are layered to create a whole that's much more complex than the sum of its parts. This braised chicken dish with earthy vegetables is built on a base of classic Puerto Rican sofrito, aromatic dried oregano and bay leaves, and tart tomato sauce and wine, then brightened with a hit of tropical golden rum and briny olives.

FRICASE DE POLLO CON PAPAS Y ZANAHORIAS
Chicken Fricassee with Potatoes and Carrots

SERVES 4

- 1 (5-pound) chicken, cut into 8 pieces
- 1 teaspoon kosher salt, plus more as needed
- ½ teaspoon freshly ground black pepper, plus more as needed
- 1 tablespoon dried oregano
- ¼ cup olive oil
- 1 cup sofrito (page 40)
- ½ cup green olives, pitted or not
- 1 cup tomato sauce
- 1 cup tomato paste
- ½ cup golden rum
- 1 cup red or white wine
- 4 bay leaves
- 6 potatoes, peeled and cut into 1-inch cubes
- 4 carrots, peeled and diced
  Hot cooked white rice (page 132), for serving
  Tostones (page 166), for serving (optional)

Season the chicken with the salt, pepper, and oregano. In a large skillet, heat the oil over medium-high heat. Add the sofrito, olives, and chicken. Cook for 5 minutes. Stir in the tomato sauce, tomato paste, rum, wine, and 2 cups water. Add the bay leaves, potatoes, and carrots and bring to a boil. Reduce the heat to a simmer and cook for 30 to 45 minutes, until the chicken and vegetables are tender. Serve with rice and maybe some tostones.

Completely addicting, these crunchy, starchy flattened disks are made by frying chunks of green plantain (they must be green), pulling them from the roiling oil, flattening them, and then dunking them back in the hot oil for a final crisping. We love to eat them solo sprinkled with salt, dunked into mayoketchup (page 65), or alongside many of our favorite main dishes.

TOSTONES
Double-Fried Green Plantains

MAKES 6 TO 8 TOSTONES

Vegetable oil, for deep-frying
1   green plantain, peeled and cut crosswise into 1-inch slices
Kosher salt

In a large skillet, heat 3 inches of oil over medium-high heat to 350°F. Line a plate with paper towels.

Carefully drop the plantain slices into the hot oil and fry on both sides for about 3 minutes. Using a slotted spoon, transfer the plantains to the paper towel–lined plate. Flatten the plantains using a tostonera (a utensil made especially for this task) or a plate or other object with a flat surface. Return the flattened slices to the hot oil and fry them again for 1 minute on each side. Remove with tongs and drain again on the paper towels. Season with salt and serve immediately.

AJILI-MOJILI / GARLIC SAUCE

This fragrant, piquant sauce is excellent served with any meat or fish as well as with *tostones*. Lots of people make this and keep it on hand as an all-purpose condiment for the table in the same way that chimichurri is used in Argentina. It's very good with our slow-roasted pork, as the sharpness of the vinegar and citrus cuts through the rich meat and skin. Some people enhance the sauce with their own additions of ingredients like capers or onions, but I like to keep it very simple and this recipe is *ajili-mojili* at it's most basic.

MAKES 2½ CUPS

6   cloves garlic
8   black peppercorns
10   ají dulce or other sweet, red peppers
½   cup white vinegar
½   cup fresh lime juice
3   teaspoons salt
1   cup olive oil

Combine the garlic, peppercorns, peppers, vinegar, lime juice, and salt in the bowl of a food processor. Process just until the peppers and garlic are finely chopped (but not pureed), about 1 minute. While the blades are turning, drizzle in the olive oil to combine completely. Transfer to a bowl and serve or cover and refrigerate for up to 1 week.

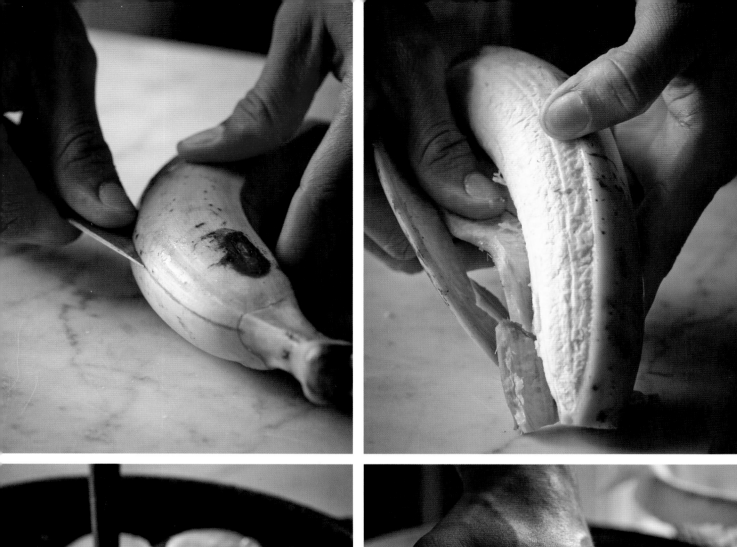

One of my goals when I set out to write this book was to not only highlight my own cooking but also present Puerto Rican cuisine in a fresh light. Traditional recipes that fall out of fashion for whatever reason are in danger of being lost if people stop cooking them. While we will always eat *arroz con pollo* or beef with rice and pink beans here, some of the old dishes that take a bit more effort could be forgotten if the recipes stop being published or passed down. This *piñón* (sort of like a lasagna without pasta) is a hearty, old-fashioned dish in which annatto-scented ground beef is layered with caramelized sweet plantains. It is an unexpected combination, and one that deserves to be more widely appreciated.

PIÑÓN DE AMARILLOS CON CARNE MOLIDA
Plantain and Beef Casserole

SERVES 6

- ½ cup plus 2 tablespoons olive oil
- 1 large onion, chopped
- 1½ pounds ground beef
- ⅓ cup chopped red bell pepper
- ⅓ cup chopped green bell pepper
- ½ teaspoon kosher salt
- ½ teaspoon freshly ground black pepper
- 2 bay leaves
- ½ teaspoon ground annatto (achiote)
- ½ cup pitted and halved green olives
- 1 tablespoon tomato paste
- 1½ tablespoons cider vinegar
- 6 very ripe sweet plantains, peeled and cut lengthwise into ⅓-inch-thick planks
- 2 large eggs
- ½ pound fresh haricots verts, blanched, or frozen French-style green beans, thawed, cut into 1-inch-long pieces

In a large skillet, heat ¼ cup of the oil over medium-high heat. Add the onion and sauté until translucent, 3 to 5 minutes. Add the beef and cook, stirring occasionally, for about 5 minutes. Add the red and green bell peppers, salt, black pepper, bay leaves, and annatto and cook until the vegetables are soft, 6 to 8 minutes. Add the olives, tomato paste, and vinegar, reduce the heat to medium, and cook, stirring occasionally, until all the excess liquid has evaporated, about 30 minutes. Let cool slightly.

In a large skillet, heat ¼ cup of the oil over medium-high heat. Add the plantains and sauté until they begin to caramelize on the edges, about 2 minutes on each side. Remove from the skillet and drain on a paper towel-lined plate.

Preheat the oven to 350°F. Grease a 10-by-12-inch or similar-size baking dish with the remaining 2 tablespoons oil.

In a small bowl, whisk the eggs and 2 tablespoons water together and set aside. Spread half of the plantains in the bottom of the prepared baking dish. Spread the beef mixture on top of the plantains. On top of the beef, evenly spread the green beans and top with the remaining plantain slices. Pour the egg mixture evenly over the top and around the sides of the plantains and bake for about 40 minutes, until the casserole is bubbling and browning on the top. Let stand for about 10 minutes before cutting into portions. Serve hot.

AN AFTERNOON
IN OLD SAN JUAN

—

MENU

—

CANAPÉ DE ARROZ A CABALLO
**Rice Fritters with Baby Bananas
and Quail Eggs, page 48**

BACALAO A LA VIZCAÍNA
Codfish Biscayan Style, page 172

FLAN DE GUANÁBANA
Soursop Custard, page 217

ALBARIÑO WINE

A SELECTION OF RUMS

My father, also called Jose, was in the restaurant business for many years. He owned several cafeterias in San Juan and one of the first pizza places on the island, Joe's Pizza House. While he wasn't the chef in any of these places, he was a good cook and enjoyed entertaining at home. One of his specialties was this classic Spanish-style codfish with capers, olives, roasted red peppers, raisins, and almonds. Leave time for soaking the cod in the refrigerator for a day.

BACALAO A LA VIZCAÍNA
Codfish Biscayan Style

SERVES 4

- 1 pound salt cod
- 1 cup milk
- 4 yellow potatoes, sliced ½ inch thick
- ¾ cup extra-virgin olive oil
- 2 onions, cut into 1-inch wedges
- ¼ cup pitted green olives, sliced
- 2 large cloves garlic, mashed to a paste in a mortar
- ¾ cup tomato paste
- ¼ cup good-quality white wine
- 2 teaspoons capers
- ½ cup peeled and sliced roasted red bell peppers (see page 142)
- 1 cup raisins
- 1 bay leaf
- 1 teaspoon smoked paprika
- 4 hard-boiled eggs, peeled and sliced
- ¼ cup sliced almonds, toasted
  Fresh parsley or culantro sprigs, for garnish

Place the salt cod in a large bowl and cover with the milk and 2 quarts water. Cover and soak in the refrigerator for 24 hours. Drain the cod, discarding the soaking liquid, and cut the fish into bite-size pieces, discarding any skin or bones.

Place the potatoes in a medium saucepan, cover with water, and bring to a boil over high heat. Reduce the heat and simmer about 10 minutes, until tender. Drain.

In a large sauté pan, heat the oil over medium heat. Add the onions, olives, garlic, and tomato paste and sauté until the onions become translucent, 7 to 10 minutes. Add 1 cup water, the wine, potatoes, capers, roasted red peppers, raisins, bay leaf, and smoked paprika and cook for about 5 minutes. Add the cod pieces and continue to cook for 10 minutes, stirring occasionally.

Garnish with the slices of hard-boiled eggs, toasted almonds, and parsley. Serve immediately.

In the shallow, warm, crystal-clear waters along Puerto Rico's shores, you can see the teeming ocean life without even putting your head in the water. One of the creatures you might see dashing around under the waves is the colorful rock lobster (also known as the Caribbean spiny lobster). The lobsters can get quite large, and, while they don't have the big claws that New England lobsters have, their tails grow especially large—and that's where the richest, sweetest meat is to be found. The tails are easy to manage and are perfect for grilling as in this recipe. It's best to purchase the lobsters live and kill them just before cooking.

LANGOSTA A LA BARBACOA CON MANTEQUILLA DE SOFRITO
Grilled Rock Lobster with Sofrito Butter

SERVES 4

4   live rock lobsters
¼   cup olive oil
      Kosher salt and freshly ground black pepper
      Juice of 1 lime
      Sofrito Butter (recipe follows)

Preheat an outdoor grill to high heat.

Place a lobster shell side down on a cutting board. Cut off the head and discard. Cut the body in half lengthwise. Remove the stomach and intestinal vein. Rinse the lobster halves. Repeat with the remaining lobsters.

Rub the lobster halves with oil, season with salt and pepper, and place on the grill, shell side down; cook for 6 minutes. Turn over and cook until the meat is just opaque in the center, about 2 minutes. Serve immediately, with a squeeze of lime juice and a dollop of sofrito butter on top.

MANTEQUILLA DE SOFRITO / SOFRITO BUTTER

MAKES 3 CUPS

1   cup sofrito (page 40), at room temperature
2   cups (4 sticks) butter, softened

In a bowl, mix together the butter and sofrito until well combined. Spoon the butter mixture onto a piece of plastic wrap and shape into a cylinder. Roll the cylinder in the plastic and fold in or twist the ends to seal. Store in the refrigerator for up to 2 weeks or freeze, tightly wrapped, for up to 2 months.

While every family puts their own little twist on potato salad, this recipe represents a very typical Puerto Rican version. Made with salty green olives, crunchy raw carrots, and hard-boiled eggs, it's the potato salad I was raised on.

ENSALADA DE PAPA
Potato Salad with Olives and Pimentos

SERVES 6 TO 8

1½ pounds potatoes, peeled and cut into ½-inch cubes
½ cup sliced green olives stuffed with pimentos
¼ cup diced fresh carrot
½ cup chopped green bell pepper
½ cup chopped yellow onion
⅓ cup diced pimentos, drained
½ teaspoon kosher salt, or more to taste
½ teaspoon freshly ground black pepper, or more to taste
½ cup mayonnaise (page 106)
4 hard-boiled eggs, peeled and chopped

Put the potatoes in a large saucepan and add cold water to cover by at least 1 inch. Bring to a boil over medium-high heat and cook until tender, about 7 minutes. Drain in a colander and immediately submerge the potatoes in a large bowl of ice water to stop the cooking. Allow the potatoes to stay in the ice water for just a couple of minutes, until cold. Drain again and spread the potatoes on a tray lined with paper towels to dry.

In a large bowl, combine the olives, carrot, bell pepper, onion, pimentos, salt, pepper, and potatoes and mix together. Gently fold in the mayonnaise and the hard-boiled eggs until combined. Taste and adjust the seasoning. The potato salad will keep, covered, in the refrigerator for up to 3 days.

This refreshing salad is perfect for a hot day and features so many of the fruits that grow everywhere on the island. Papaya is indigenous to Puerto Rico, and avocado, oranges, and grapefruit grow prolifically here, too. Many Puerto Ricans have all of these trees growing in their yards, so putting these ingredients all together in a salad with just a simple dressing of lime juice and olive oil follows naturally.

ENSALADA DE AGUACATE, PAPAYA, CHINA Y TORONJA
Avocado and Papaya Salad

SERVES 8

2   avocados, peeled and cut into 8 wedges each
2   ripe papayas, peeled and cut into ½-inch-thick slices
1   navel orange, peeled and cut into segments
1   grapefruit, peeled and cut into segments
¼   cup olive oil
2   tablespoons fresh lime juice
    Kosher salt and freshly ground black pepper
8   fresh mint leaves
3   tablespoons chopped fresh cilantro

Arrange the avocado, papaya, orange, and grapefruit decoratively on a flat tray or serving dish. Sprinkle the oil and lime juice over the fruit and season with salt and pepper to taste. Tear the mint leaves and mix with the cilantro. Scatter the herbs over the top of the fruit and serve immediately or cover and refrigerate for up to 1 hour.

POSTRES

Desserts

Buñuelos are old-fashioned Puerto Rican sweets that are not made very often anymore—a situation I'm dedicated to changing. We make these delicate fritters in a tangerine-scented syrup in our restaurant not only because they're delicious, but also because they're becoming so hard to find these days and seem to be in danger of disappearing from the repertoire altogether.

BUÑUELOS DE VIENTO EN ALMÍBAR DE MANDARINA Y ANÍS
Light-as-Air Fritters in Tangerine and Anise Syrup

SERVES 6

FOR THE FRITTERS:
1 cup (2 sticks) butter, cut into pieces
  Pinch of kosher salt
2 cups all-purpose flour
8 large eggs
  Vegetable oil, for deep-frying

FOR THE TANGERINE AND ANISE SYRUP:
6 cups granulated sugar
1 vanilla bean, split in half lengthwise
1 strip of tangerine, mandarin orange, or clementine zest removed with a vegetable peeler, plus 2 tablespoons grated zest
3 star anise pods
1 cinnamon stick

MAKE THE FRITTERS: In a large, heavy pot, heat at least 3 inches of oil to 350°F. Line a plate with paper towels.

Meanwhile, in a medium saucepan, combine 2 cups water, the butter, and the salt and bring to a boil. Remove from the heat, then whisk in the flour all at once until well blended. Drop in the eggs one at a time, mixing until combined after each is added before adding the next.

When the oil is hot, drop in the batter by tablespoons and deep-fry until golden brown, 3 to 4 minutes. Using a slotted spoon, transfer the fritters to the paper towel-lined plate.

MAKE THE TANGERINE AND ANISE SYRUP: In a saucepan, combine the sugar, vanilla bean, strip of tangerine zest, star anise, cinnamon stick, and 8 cups water and bring to a boil over high heat. Cook until the syrup becomes a bit thick, 10 to 12 minutes. Remove from the heat. Add the grated zest to the syrup.

Place the buñuelos in a large bowl or into individual bowls and pour the anise syrup on top, preferably while the buñuelos are still hot as then they will best absorb the syrup. You can prepare the buñuelos, letting them soak in the syrup, up to 5 hours in advance of serving. The buñuelos and syrup are best served at room temperature, but you may like them chilled as well.

Glistening and perfectly white, this dessert is called *tembleque*, which translates to "tremble." It gets the name from its lovely, panna cotta–like texture and the way it trembles with movement. The dessert can be served elegantly from individual ramekins or made in a larger vessel and spooned out. This beautiful coconut pudding is one of Puerto Rico's most beloved Christmas desserts.

TEMBLEQUE
Coconut Milk Pudding

SERVES 8

4   cups fresh coconut milk (recipe follows)
⅔   cup sugar
½   cup cornstarch
½   teaspoon kosher salt
1   strip orange zest removed with a vegetable peeler (with as little white pith as possible)
1   tablespoon fresh orange juice
    Ground cinnamon, for garnish

In a medium saucepan, combine the coconut milk, sugar, cornstarch, salt, and orange zest. Cook over medium-high heat, stirring continuously with a wooden spoon, until the mixture starts to thicken. Reduce the heat to medium and continue stirring until the mixture comes to a boil. Remove from the heat and stir in the orange juice. Discard the orange zest and pour the mixture into an aluminum pan or individual ramekins; let cool for about 30 minutes, then place in the refrigerator to chill completely, about 3 hours.

If using a large pan, sprinkle with cinnamon and spoon out to serve; if using ramekins, loosen the edges with a knife and turn each tembleque out onto an individual serving plate and sprinkle with cinnamon.

Coconuts grow high above us in the lush palms that dot the entire island. Both in the city and rural areas, climbers collect the fruit to sell in markets and on street corners. Cracking the fruit open is a celebratory ritual; it is impossible to open the fruit quietly. Once the hard shell is breached, delicious and healthy coconut water flows freely—ready to drink. Removing the flesh from the inner surface of the shell takes a little effort, but the meat holds flavorful potential as a snack straight from the source or processed in ways that render it a vehicle for both sweet and savory recipes.

Coconut milk (different from the fresh water that flows out) is obtained by soaking the grated, firm flesh of the fruit in the collected coconut water. Once the shreds are saturated completely, they are strained through a cheesecloth. The resulting milk delivers concentrated coconut flavor in a silky texture that mingles very well with acidic fruit and can tame intense heat and spicy flavors.

The water content of a coconut varies depending on the fruit's age and ripeness. Green coconuts carry the most water, but their flesh is not suitable for grating. You want the hard, brown, totally ripe coconuts in order to get firm flesh suitable for grating. For this recipe, if you do not get enough coconut water from a brown coconut, you can supplement it by cracking another green or brown coconut or by using storebought coconut water.

LECHE DE COCO FRESCA / FRESH COCONUT MILK

MAKES 4 CUPS

2 coconuts

To open the coconuts, you will need a hammer. Hold one coconut over a large bowl with the three "eyes" (the darker brown spots on one side) facing toward you. Imagine an equator around the circumference of the fruit and strike the coconut with a robust blow on that invisible equator line, being careful to avoid your fingers. Continue striking the coconut along that line while turning the fruit a bit after each blow. This will take several strikes and may even require you to rotate the coconut a few times completely before you hear a deep cracking sound. At this point, the coconut water will gush out and empty out into the bowl. You should have about 2 ½ cups of coconut water.

Once the coconut is cracked open, use your hands or the hammer to break the shell into several smaller, more manageable pieces. Use a paring knife to free the white flesh from the brown shell, discarding the shell. Grate the flesh with a box grater. You should have approximately 5 cups of grated coconut.

In a saucepan, combine 2 ½ cups water and the coconut water and bring to a boil over medium-high heat. Stir in the grated coconut and remove from the heat. Let cool for about 1 hour.

Strain the mixture through a fine-mesh sieve lined with a layer of cheesecloth set over a bowl, squeezing out as much liquid as possible. The coconut milk can be used immediately or covered and stored in the refrigerator for up to 2 days (freezing is not recommended).

COFFEE

The uplifting scent of freshly pulled espresso wafts through the streets of every town in Puerto Rico.

An important part of our culture, coffee was once a pillar of the island's economy. The area of the central mountain range, La Cordillera Central, offers the rich soil and proper elevation that make for the plant's ideal growing conditions. Historically, this beautiful region—which is also one of Earth's most biodiverse landscapes—was dotted by haciendas, or coffee plantations. In the 1890s, Puerto Rico was the world's fourth-largest producer.

A lush, full bush, the coffee plant flowers and then produces what is called a "cherry" because of its bright red color when ripe. The cherries form in clusters that cling tightly along each branch, and since the berries on each branch ripen at different times, the same bush must be picked about three different times over the course of a few weeks in the harvest season.

Harvesters wash the cherries and extract the seeds (what we call the coffee beans). It is the seed that then goes through a process of fermentation and drying before its outer husk is removed. At this point the beans are tossed into a roaster where they will be monitored carefully until they uniformly reach the proper temperature, turning from green to a light brown or mahogany hue. In Puerto Rico, we generally favor a dark roast.

Because harvesting coffee is such back-breaking work, it has become increasingly difficult to find pickers willing to work for the standard wages. In the last fifteen years, the number of coffee farms has shrunk by more than half here. But, the recent "coffee culture" movement that prizes high-quality, fair trade, and single estate beans, may offer hope for growers. The University of Puerto Rico in Utuado has built a coffee laboratory where students can learn the art and science of growing, harvesting, and roasting coffee as well as techniques for marketing one of Puerto Rico's most delicious products. When visiting the island, do as the natives do and order either an espresso ("*café*"), *cortadito* (espresso with a small layer of steamed milk), or a *café con leche* (equal parts espresso and steamed milk).

Every once in a while a dish takes the world by storm and ends up, in some form or another, on just about every restaurant menu. It might have been developed years before (the details of its origin are disputed), but when chef Jean-Georges Vongerichten put his now-classic molten chocolate cake on the menu at JoJo in New York, people went nuts. This tropical version of that glorious cake is one of the most popular desserts at my own restaurant. Very sweet baby banana slices are baked in the middle of the warm, slightly underbaked chocolate cake, giving it a taste of Puerto Rico. It's especially delicious served with nutmeg and vanilla ice cream.

BIZCOCHO DE CHOCOLATE RELLENO DE GUINEITOS NIÑOS
Warm Chocolate Cake Filled with Baby Bananas

SERVES 6

- 1 cup (2 sticks) unsalted butter, softened and cut into small pieces, plus more for the ramekins
- 8 ounces good-quality bittersweet chocolate, chopped (1 cup)
- 4 large eggs
- 4 egg yolks
- ⅔ cup granulated sugar, plus more for dusting
- ¼ cup all-purpose flour
- 3 baby bananas, or 2 ripe standard bananas, sliced ½ inch thick
  Confectioners' sugar, for dusting
  Nutmeg and Vanilla Ice Cream (recipe follows on page 192)

Preheat the oven to 450°F. Butter six 6-ounce ramekins and lightly dust them with sugar, shaking out any excess.

In a heatproof bowl set over a saucepan of simmering water (making sure the bowl does not touch the water), heat the butter and chocolate, stirring continuously, until the chocolate is completely melted and the mixture is well combined. Remove from the heat and set aside to cool slightly.

In a separate bowl, beat together the whole eggs, egg yolks, and sugar with a whisk or electric mixer until pale yellow in color and thick. Pour the cooled chocolate into the egg mixture, whisking as you pour. Stir in the flour until combined.

Divide half of the batter evenly among the six ramekins. Distribute the banana slices in a single layer among the ramekins and cover them evenly with the remaining chocolate batter. Place the ramekins on a baking sheet and bake for 8 minutes. Remove from the oven, let cool for a couple of minutes, then turn the little cakes out onto individual serving dishes. (Alternatively, you can put the batter and bananas in the ramekins for baking ahead of time. Cover them with plastic wrap and store in the refrigerator for up to 24 hours. When ready to bake, remove the plastic, place on a baking sheet, and bake at 450°F for 10 minutes.)

Serve warm, dusted with confectioners' sugar, with the ice cream.

HELADO DE NUEZ MOSCADA Y VAINILLA / NUTMEG AND VANILLA ICE CREAM

**MAKES 1 QUART,
6 TO 8 SERVINGS**

2 cups heavy cream
½ cup whole milk
1 vanilla bean, split in half
   lengthwise
2 teaspoons freshly grated
   nutmeg
4 egg yolks
¼ cup granulated sugar
3 tablespoons simple syrup
   (see page 235)

Fill a large bowl with ice water and set aside. In a saucepan, combine the cream, milk, vanilla bean, and 1 teaspoon of the nutmeg. Bring to a boil over medium-high heat, then immediately remove from the heat. In a separate bowl, beat the egg yolks and sugar together with an electric mixer until pale yellow in color and thickened.

Remove the vanilla bean from the cream mixture (discard it or save it for another use). Slowly add about ¼ cup of the warm cream to the egg yolk mixture while stirring continuously to temper the eggs. Return the mixture to the saucepan of the warm cream mixture. Place over medium heat and cook until the mixture is thick enough to coat the back of a spoon, 2 to 3 minutes. Remove from the heat and add the simple syrup. Strain through a fine-mesh sieve into a bowl, then add the remaining 1 teaspoon nutmeg and set the bowl in the bowl of ice water to cool the custard. Transfer the custard to an ice cream machine and process according to the manufacturer's instructions. Transfer to an airtight container and freeze until ready to serve.

Opposite: The Cathedral of San Juan Bautista, amidst the skyline of Old San Juan.

The people of Puerto Rico don't need to wait for a holiday to have a party. Food, drink, music, friends, and family are important to us and we enjoy a culture of continual celebration.

Parties are common, whether there is a special occasion or not, so when a big holiday rolls around the celebration is huge. Christmastime celebrations in Puerto Rico begin at least a month before the day itself. One tradition that is unique to the island is the *parranda*, when friends gather together to practice musical numbers and then head out to surprise an unsuspecting friend with a performance. It's sort of like Christmas caroling but more lively and a little mischievous: The surprise visit typically takes place late at night in order to wake the lucky beneficiary. It's not just singing, either; there might be guitars, tambourines, maracas, and more—whatever it takes to make it loud and joyful! After the music, a full-blown party generally breaks out with food, more music, and dancing into the night.

There are typical foods associated with Christmas in Puerto Rico as well. It really wouldn't be Christmas without roast pig cooked on a spit over smoldering coals. Some people may head to a *lechonera* (see page 82) to enjoy their pork, but there are those who make an entire day of cooking the pig outside on a rotating spit (either mechanical or turned by hand). It takes many hours to slow-roast the pig, so building a party out of the cooking process is typical. Friends and family will bring other holiday treats like *pasteles* (page 151), *morcilla* (page 31), and *tembleque* (page 184) for the feast, which usually takes place on Christmas Eve, or Nochebuena. We also have our own version of eggnog called *coquito*, made with coconut and rum (page 246).

Children are always excited to open presents, but traditionally it is not Santa Claus who delivers gifts to the children but rather Los Reyes Magos, the three kings who visited the baby Jesus and brought gifts. Families will exchange gifts with each other on Christmas Day, but January 6 is the day of the Three Kings, which carries our celebration beyond New Year's parties into the first week of January.

Coconuts are everywhere on this island: in the markets, at roadside stands, in the trees. This very simple dish is an old favorite, found in most traditional Puerto Rican cookbooks. *Cocada* is one of the first recipes that children learn to cook here because it is so easy—it's a great way for kids to start learning their way around the kitchen. Delicious and satisfying, *cocada* is always on the menu at Santaella.

•

COCADA
Coconut and Almond Soufflé

SERVES 4 TO 6

4   cups canned grated coconut in heavy syrup
     (e de coco)
     espoons (½ stick) butter, melted
     e eggs, beaten
     sliced almonds

Preheat the oven to 350°F. Butter a 9-by-13-inch baking dish or six 6-ounce ramekins or flan dishes.

In a large bowl, combine the coconut, butter, and eggs and mix well. Pour into the prepared baking dish and sprinkle the top with the almonds. Bake until the top is golden and the almonds become a bit toasty, about 20 minutes. Serve hot.

I have good memories of visiting my relatives in the hilly, central part of the island when I was a child. The lifestyle was so different than in San Juan—acres of land to play on and a verdant backdrop that was a stark contrast to the bustling city.

Tamarind trees grow all over the countryside in Puerto Rico. The strange-looking trees produce long, brown seedpods (see page 209); the outside of the pods becomes dark brown and crunchy when the gooey pulp that surrounds the seeds inside is at its fullest and sweetest. I loved them as a kid and after a day of picking and opening the pods, my hands and mouth would be dark with the sticky fruit. The sweet, slightly tannic pulp is the perfect complement to the sesame seeds and vanilla in this ice cream.

HELADO DE VAINILLA Y AJONJOLÍ EN JUGO DE TAMARINDO
Sesame Seed and Vanilla Ice Cream in Tamarind Juice

**MAKES ABOUT 1 QUART,
6 TO 8 SERVINGS**

2   cups heavy cream
1   cup whole milk
3   teaspoons sesame seed paste
    (either tahini or Japanese sesame
    paste)
4   egg yolks
½   cup granulated sugar
1   tablespoon mixed white and
    black sesame seeds, toasted,
    plus more for garnish
2   teaspoons good-quality vanilla
    extract
2   cups tamarind juice (recipe
    follows), chilled

Fill a large bowl with ice water and set aside. In a saucepan, combine the cream, milk, and 1 teaspoon of the sesame seed paste. Bring to a boil over medium-high heat, then immediately remove from the heat.

In a medium bowl, beat together the egg yolks and sugar with an electric mixer until pale yellow in color and thickened. While mixing on low speed, slowly add some of the warm cream mixture to the egg mixture to temper the eggs. Pour the egg mixture into the saucepan with the warm cream mixture and cook over medium heat until thick enough to coat the back of a spoon, 2 to 3 minutes. Remove from the heat and pour into a clean bowl. Stir in the remaining 2 teaspoons sesame seed paste. Add the sesame seeds and set the bowl over the bowl of ice water to cool.

Transfer to an ice cream machine and process according to the manufacturer's instructions. Transfer to an airtight container and freeze until ready to serve. Pour about 1 inch of tamarind juice in the bottom of each individual serving bowl. Place a scoop of ice cream in each bowl with the juice and serve immediately, sprinkled with more sesame seeds.

JUGO DE TAMARINDO / TAMARIND JUICE

MAKES 4 CUPS

1   pound tamarind seeds with their pulp
2   cups granulated sugar
3   tablespoons fresh lemon juice

In a saucepan, combine the tamarind with 5 cups water and bring to a boil over medium-high heat. Cook at a gentle boil for about 10 minutes. Remove from the heat and strain through a colander set over a bowl; discard the solids. Add the sugar and lemon juice to the liquid and mix well. Cover and refrigerate until ready to use. The mixture will keep for up to 1 week.

My grandmother on my mother's side was famous for this custardlike dessert. It is a very typical traditional recipe: Mashed *calabaza*, sweet potatoes, and sweet plantains are mixed with eggs and a spice infusion and baked in a dish lined with plantain leaves, which give the custard an aromatic, earthy rusticity.

CAZUELA DE CALABAZA Y BATATA
Pumpkin and Sweet Potato Casserole

SERVES 12

2   pounds calabaza (see page 27, or pumpkin), peeled, seeded, and cut into 2-inch chunks

2   pounds batatas (see page 27) or sweet potatoes, peeled and cut into 2-inch chunks

1   pound ripe sweet plantains, peeled

2   teaspoons kosher salt

2   cinnamon sticks

1   star anise pod

2   tablespoons grated, peeled fresh ginger

4   whole cloves

    Plantain or banana leaves (thawed, if frozen)

5   tablespoons butter, softened, plus more for the baking dish

4   large eggs

2   cups granulated sugar

2½ tablespoons all-purpose flour

2½ tablespoons rice flour

1   cup fresh coconut milk (page 187)

In a large saucepan, combine the pumpkin, sweet potatoes, plantains, and 1 teaspoon of the salt and cover with at least 2 inches of water. Bring to a boil over medium-high heat and cook until the pumpkin and sweet potatoes are soft, about 30 minutes.

In a small saucepan, combine the cinnamon sticks, star anise, ginger, and cloves with 1 cup water. Cover and bring to a boil over high heat, then immediately remove from the heat and allow the water and spices to infuse for 20 minutes. Strain the spice-infused water in a sieve set over a bowl and reserve the liquid.

Preheat the oven to 350°F. Butter the bottom and sides of a 9-by-13-inch baking dish, line the bottom and the sides with plantain leaves, and butter the leaves.

Drain the pumpkin, sweet potatoes, and plantains and mash them with a potato masher until they are the texture of mashed potatoes. Stir in the butter, eggs, and sugar, then add the spice-infused liquid. Stir in the all-purpose flour, rice flour, the remaining 1 teaspoon salt, and the coconut milk. Pour the pumpkin mixture into the prepared dish and bake for 2 hours, or until set. Let cool to room temperature before serving. The casserole is also good served chilled.

Mampostial is a very classic confection from Puerto Rico. These candies are commonly found prepackaged in sweets shops, but it's easy to make your own. Two ingredients—sugarcane molasses and fresh grated coconut—are cooked down, poured out to cool, and cut into pieces. Wrap them in waxed paper to give as gifts.

MAMPOSTIAL
Coconut Molasses Chews

MAKES 6 BARS

1½ cups molasses
1½ cups freshly grated coconut

In a saucepan, combine the molasses and coconut. Cook over low heat, stirring continuously with a wooden spoon, until the mixture thickens and separates from the sides of the saucepan, 15 to 20 minutes. Turn out onto a greased platter or a slab of marble. Let cool to room temperature, then cut into rectangles about 1 by 2 inches. These can be stored, individually wrapped in waxed paper, at room temperature for up to 1 month.

This is a creative way to serve an individual chocolate mousse: in a flowerpot with a coffee-flavored crumble that looks like dirt. You can get creative, adding sprigs of mint or edible flowers to the "soil" or inserting wooden popsicle sticks (resembling garden seed markers) with names of guests written on them.

TIERRITA
Chocolate and Coffee "Soil" in Clay Pots

SERVES 6

FOR THE MOUSSE:

1½ cups chopped bittersweet chocolate
3 large eggs
¼ cup granulated sugar
1 teaspoon good-quality unsweetened cocoa powder
1½ cups heavy cream

FOR THE "SOIL":

½ cup granulated sugar
½ cup macadamia nuts
1 teaspoon kosher salt
¼ cup all-purpose flour
2 tablespoons ground coffee beans
5 tablespoons butter, melted
8 Oreo cookies
6 large fresh mint sprigs

MAKE THE MOUSSE: Put the chocolate in a heatproof bowl set over a saucepan of simmering water (be sure the bottom of the bowl isn't touching the water) and stir the chocolate occasionally until melted. Remove from the heat and let cool for a few minutes.

Put the eggs and sugar in a bowl and beat with an electric mixer until the mixture is pale yellow in color and thick. Stir the cooled chocolate and the cocoa powder into the egg mixture until mixed well. In a separate bowl, whip the cream until soft peaks form. Gently fold the whipped cream into the chocolate mixture until combined. Pour into the clay pots, cover, and refrigerate for at least 2 hours or up to 5 days.

MAKE THE "SOIL": Preheat the oven to 350°F. Line a baking sheet with parchment paper.

In a food processor, grind together the sugar, macadamia nuts, salt, flour, and coffee until fine. Add the melted butter to the mixture and pulse a couple of times to mix well. Spread the mixture onto the prepared baking sheet and bake for 10 to 12 minutes, until the mixture is set and lightly toasted. Let cool completely.

In the food processor, process the cookies until crumbly and mix them into the baked "soil" mixture. The "soil" can be made up to 1 week in advance and stored in an airtight container.

Pour the soil on top of the chocolate mousse mixture in the clay pots to look like potting soil. Insert a mint sprig in the middle of each to emulate a little seedling. Serve.

NOTE: You will need six clay pots, about 3 inches deep and 4 inches across the top. These hold ¾ cup of the mousse plus the "soil" that gets sprinkled on top.

When I was a little boy, I loved going to fancy restaurants and watching the elegant waiters cook cherries jubilee tableside. I was mesmerized by the show, and even though the dish is considered to be a bit difficult to pull off, it was one of the first I learned how to cook as a boy. I enjoy taking classic European-style dishes like this and giving them a tropical twist. Here I include mamey, which is a small tropical fruit in the same family as *sapote*. It grows on very large trees and has unremarkable brown skin but beautiful orange flesh.

JUBILEE DE MAMEY Y PIÑA
Tropical Fruit Jubilee

SERVES 6

½ cup (1 stick) butter, cut into pieces
1 cup diced peeled pineapple
1 ripe mamey, peeled and diced
½ teaspoon ground cinnamon
½ cup granulated sugar
¼ cup dark rum
¼ cup brandy
  Vanilla ice cream, for serving

In a nonstick skillet, melt the butter over medium-high heat. When the butter is melted and bubbling, add the pineapple and mamey and cook, stirring occasionally, for about 4 minutes. Add the cinnamon and sugar and stir well. Cook until the pineapple starts to brown slightly, 2 to 5 minutes more. Add the rum and brandy, tilting the skillet so that the flame from the burner touches the alcohol (or use a long lighter to light the alcohol) and flambé for a couple of seconds (the flame will burn out quickly). Transfer to individual plates and serve immediately with a scoop of ice cream over each.

FRUTAS

TROPICAL FRUITS

Gorgeous tropical fruits are abundant on the island, and even in the busiest parts of our largest cities you'll find fruit trees growing on small patches of land and in the yards around houses.

In most parts of the United States, many of these fruits are a real luxury item and can be expensive. Here, there are often too many citrus fruits, mango, and papaya to even use before they fall to the ground.

AVOCADO This delicious and healthful fruit is actually not sweet and is rarely used in desserts. The avocados that are typical here are different from the California Haas avocados and have a brighter, cooler taste. They're more like the Fuerte variety that is often grown in Florida. Avocado should always be used ripe and should be peeled and the pit removed. The flesh can turn dark very quickly once it is cut, so it is a good idea to have some lemon or lime juice ready to sprinkle over it to slow the oxidation process, and to cut avocado just before you plan to serve it.

BANANA *Guineo,* as they're called in Spanish, are everywhere in Puerto Rico, and we use them in all forms for our dishes. There are several varieties including the common medium- to large-sized bananas that you can pick up in any supermarket. We use these in their green, unripe form in savory dishes such as the Pickled Green Bananas on page 109. There are very small bananas that we call *guineitos niños,* which are very sweet and have a strong concentrated banana flavor—almost like banana candy. And there are some called *guineos manzanos* that taste a bit like apple when they are ripe. Ripe, yellow bananas and baby bananas are enjoyed plain and are also used in desserts, from simple fruit salads to more sophisticated dishes like the Warm Chocolate Cake Filled with Baby Bananas (page 191), one of the most popular dishes at Santaella.

CITRUS The range of flavors that the citrus fruits of the world provide is vast. The standard oranges, grapefruits, lemons, and limes that you find in a grocery store are a poor reflection of the profiles that can be achieved by stretching beyond hybridized, mass-market citrus. Trees laden with all sorts of varieties of citrus fruits grow all over Puerto Rico, and the homegrown fruits are generally much better than anything you will find in a grocery store. It is easy to find the usual varieties but also some that are less common, like the *chironja,* which is a cross between an orange and a grapefruit, and bitter orange, also known as sour orange or Seville orange. Bitter oranges, which are not nearly as sweet as regular eating oranges, were brought to the Caribbean from Spain, but their origins are in Southeast Asia. They are becoming easier to find in the States and if you do see some, grab them and start experimenting with the juice. If you need a substitution, try blending equal parts regular orange juice and lime juice.

COCONUT One of the most common ingredients in our food and drink culture is coconut. The trees are everywhere,

and it's not unusual to see men climbing the trees—even in the city—to pick coconuts. They are sold in markets, roadside stands, and even from boxes and shopping carts on street corners. Both green (young) and brown (old) coconuts are used in Puerto Rico. The green coconuts have not yet developed their rock-hard, brown hairy shell and are softer and have much more water inside. The flesh of a green coconut is gelatinous and not yet mature and therefore does not have much flavor. Older brown coconuts have matured. Most of the water is gone from the inside and as the flesh has matured and concentrated so has the flavor of the meat. Green coconuts are hacked open for fresh coconut water, and the flesh of the brown fruit is used in both sweet and savory dishes.

GUAVA Native to the Caribbean islands as well as Mexico and Central and South America, the guava is a prolific plant that spreads easily in the wild but has also become an important cultivar in tropical locales worldwide. There are many varieties ranging from golf-ball-sized strawberry guavas to softball-sized apple guavas. Starting off as a green fruit, some stay green throughout their life while others turn yellow and some maroon. The color of the flesh varies as well, but the guavas in Puerto Rico are mostly a beautiful rosy color. They can be eaten raw (some varieties, like the apple guava, can be eaten like an apple—skin and all); their flavor is a sort of citrusy, apple-strawberry combination, and their texture when ripe is soft but not mushy. They are very nutritious, boasting four times the amount of vitamin C as an orange! Because they contain a high level of pectin, we make candies, jams, and fruit pastes out of them. Guava paste can be used for cooking but also makes a delicious accompaniment to a cheese board. Try the Cream Cheese and Vanilla Panna Cotta with Guava Filling on page 225.

MAMEY Beautiful dark green, glossy leaves adorn the mamey tree, which grows very well and quite large in Puerto Rico. Some people plant them as an ornamental tree—they look similar to the grand Southern magnolia. The mamey tree has the additional benefit of bearing a delicious fruit that we use in jams and pastes, blend into smoothies and milk shakes, and cook into desserts like the Tropical Fruit Jubilee with Pineapple and Mamey on page 204. The apricot-like flavor of the semifirm mamey flesh is delicious raw and offers many nutrients, like vitamins B and C, and a good amount of dietary fiber. Native to the West Indies, it is a New World fruit that doesn't like too much change. While it grows very well in Puerto Rico and in South and Central America, cultivating the fruit in the tropical areas of the Old World have not proven very successful: The mamey is a stubborn beauty. The good news is that Puerto Rico enjoys some of the most productive mamey trees in the world, with some trees producing crops biannually—that's three to four hundred fruits per tree each year!

MANGO Native to Southeast Asia and brought to the islands via Spanish exploration and African slave ships, the mango is a fruit tree that has adapted well to our land. They range from small and bright yellow to larger, reddish, spherical fruits to elongated green-skinned mangoes that are very large. Mangoes have a delicious peachy-pineapple-flavored flesh; some varieties have a fibrous texture and some have no fiber at all. The delicious yellow to deep salmon-colored flesh clings to a large pit that can be nearly impossible to release, so the best way to cut a mango is to slice it on either side of the flat pit, as close to the pit as possible, to obtain two cup-shaped halves. You can then peel it or score it with a knife to create cubes that can be cut from the skin.

SOURSOP Called *guanábana* in Spanish, soursop is an unusual fruit that looks intimidating as it is covered in small spikes, but it has a mild, almost creamy white pulp inside that tastes a little bit like a combination of strawberry and pineapple. It has a citrusy sourness that is really nice when paired with syrups or sugary desserts or used in a cocktail. Native to the Caribbean, the soursop is also related to the cherimoya and the pawpaw.

PAPAYA These oblong fruits, native to the island, can be yellow or orange-red on the outside and inside. They have a lovely mild taste and texture similar to some melons, but they grow on trees in large clusters. They should be peeled, leaving the sweet, dense flesh to be eaten. When the fruit is cut in half, many black seeds will be revealed, but they are concentrated in the middle so they're easy to remove. Considered to be a power food by many, papayas contain enzymes that aid digestion and are rich in vitamins A and C as well as fiber and potassium.

PINEAPPLE An iconic fruit native to southern Brazil and Paraguay and brought throughout South America and the Caribbean by the Indians of those regions, the pineapple, apart from being sweet and delicious in desserts, savory dishes, and cocktails, is also an ancient symbol of hospitality. Taíno Indians of the Caribbean were said to hang the fruits over their doors to let visitors know that they were welcome. The fruit and the symbol was adopted by the European explorers, taken back to Europe and eventually to the colonies in North America. Some American cities that were former colonies still use the symbol today. There are a few varieties grown in Puerto Rico. Perhaps

the most popular here is the medium-sized Spanish Reds, which have a classic, deep flavor—a perfect blend of tangy and sweet. Then there are the Smooth Cayennes (the Hawaiian cultivar that is most often sold in mainland supermarkets). While they are easy to grow (and therefore have become popular on large farms), they are not the best for flavor and texture. We also have huge Cabezonas pineapples that grow as large as fifteen pounds each, and some small and delicious pineapples called Pan de Azúcar that are difficult to grow and therefore a coveted variety.

QUENEPA Bunches of these Key lime–sized green fruits, still clinging to their stems, are sold in markets and from roadside stands all over the island. Sometimes called the Spanish lime or genip fruit, quenepa are mostly eaten raw but can be used to make jams, fruit paste, and juice. The city of Ponce, on the south end of the island, hosts the Festival Nacional de la Quenepa every August, with typical street-style music, arts, and crafts but also a recipe contest with prizes going to the most delicious and innovative use of the tropical fruit. The fruits have a bright green, firm skin that is not edible. To eat one, first bite a slit into the skin with your front teeth. Once you have made a slit, you can peel the fruit easily with your fingers to reveal a round, gelatinous-looking mass of pulp that surrounds a large seed. Pop the entire thing in your mouth, and begin sucking the tart-sweet pulp that clings to the large seed. Discard the seed and eat another one!

TAMARIND It's the pulp surrounding the large seeds in this unusual pod that provides the edible portion of this fruit and the distinct tannic and pleasantly sour flavor. An import from India, tamarind trees grow very well in the Caribbean and tamarind is a common ingredient here. The seed pods have to reach the stage where their papery skin is dry and crumbly before they will have developed enough sugars to eat. Even still, once the pulp is extracted, sugar is usually added to calm its sour nature. It is fun to eat tamarind pulp directly from the pod, the dark, sticky sweetness heightened by a bit of lip puckering. Kids love to eat them for the sensation, but eat too many and your mouth will feel raw!

Previous page, clockwise from top left: Bitter orange; tamarind; mamey; mango; pineapple; mangos Mayagüezanos; chinas, a Puerto Rican variety of orange; papaya; quenepas (center left); soursop; passion fruit (cut, with green center); orange.

Crisps and cobblers are classic homey American desserts in which fruit—usually apples, stone fruit, or berries—is baked until bubbly and juicy under a topping of some sort. In this crisp, topped with a traditional oat-and-nut crumble, I use tropical mangoes, their honey-sweetness offset with plenty of fresh lemon juice. When choosing mangoes, judge by feel as opposed to color: Mangoes should be heavy for their size, and when squeezed the flesh should give slightly. Ripe specimens will often have a nice fruity aroma at the stem ends.

MANGÓ CON CUBIERTA CRUJIENTE
Mango Crisp

SERVES 4

- ¼ cup old-fashioned rolled oats
- ½ cup walnuts, chopped
- ⅓ cup brown sugar
- 1 tablespoon plus ¼ cup granulated sugar
- 1 tablespoon all-purpose flour
- ½ teaspoon ground cinnamon
- 5 tablespoons butter, melted, plus 2 tablespoons for cooking the mango
- 2½ cups diced ripe mango
- 3 tablespoons fresh lemon juice

Preheat the oven to 350°F.

In a medium bowl, stir together the oats, walnuts, brown sugar, 1 tablespoon of the granulated sugar, the flour, and the cinnamon. Pour the melted butter over the mixture and mix well using your hands.

In a nonstick skillet, melt the remaining 2 tablespoons butter over medium-high heat. Add the diced mango and remaining ¼ cup granulated sugar and cook for 4 to 5 minutes, until golden brown and caramelized. Remove from the heat and stir in the lemon juice.

Spoon the mango into individual shallow dessert dishes, or into a 9-by-9-inch baking dish, and top it evenly with the oat mixture. Bake until the topping is golden brown and crisp, about 20 minutes. Serve hot.

DULCE DE LECHOSA
Papaya Preserves

This is a wonderful tropical confiture (pictured at left) that is delicious eaten with cheese, spread onto bread, or spooned onto ice cream.

MAKES 4 CUPS

¼   cup baking soda
4   pounds peeled and seeded green papaya, cut into ¼-inch slices
8   cups granulated sugar
4   cinnamon sticks

In a large bowl, combine 10 cups water, the baking soda, and the papaya and soak for about 1 hour at room temperature. This process will make the outside of the papaya crisp while keeping the inside soft. Drain and rinse the papaya well.

In a large saucepan, combine the papaya and sugar, cover, and cook for 30 minutes over low heat. Add a little water if it starts to look too dry. Add the cinnamon sticks, stir, and cook, uncovered, for 1 hour. Let cool, then transfer to a covered container and store in the refrigerator for up to 1 month.

JALEA DE PIÑA
Pineapple Jam

This jam can be used in either sweet or savory dishes and is delicious eaten with cheese—especially Puerto Rican queso del país.

MAKES ABOUT 1½ CUPS

1   cup very finely diced peeled fresh pineapple
3   tablespoons butter
1½ cups light brown sugar
1   teaspoon balsamic vinegar

Combine all the ingredients in a medium saucepan. Heat over medium-low heat, stirring often with a wooden spoon, for about 35 minutes, until it has reduced by about half and become a bit thick. Remove from the heat and let cool. Store in an airtight container in the refrigerator for up to 3 weeks.

My grandfather was a good cook, and after he retired, he always made bread pudding. If he knew that my sister and I would be visiting he made sure to make one without raisins because my sister hated them. I honestly can't remember a time when we visited that he didn't have bread pudding, so it became something that we really craved when we knew we were headed his way. This is my version—a little more complicated than his, but always made to honor my grandfather.

BUDÍN DE PAN Y FRUTAS
Bread and Fruit Pudding

SERVES 6

This recipe is baked in a baking dish that has been "caramelized": There is a melted sugar coating in the bottom and up the sides of the pan in which the pudding is baked.

2   cups granulated sugar
4   cups milk
1   cup coconut milk
6   large eggs, beaten
2   tablespoons good-quality vanilla extract
½   teaspoon kosher salt
½   cup (1 stick) melted butter
1   cup mashed ripe bananas
1   cup dried cranberries
1   teaspoon ground cinnamon
8   cups coarsely chopped leftover bread, cake, or doughnuts, or a combination
    Rum and Vanilla Cream Sauce (recipe follows), for serving

In a saucepan, combine 1 cup of the sugar and ½ cup water and cook over medium-high heat, stirring often, until the sugar has dissolved completely. Reduce the heat to medium and cook until the syrup turns golden brown. Pour the caramel into a 9-by-13-inch baking dish and tilt the disk so the caramel coats the bottom and halfway up the sides.

Preheat the oven to 350°F.

In a large bowl, combine the remaining 1 cup sugar, the milk, coconut milk, eggs, vanilla, salt, melted butter, bananas, cranberries, and cinnamon and mix well. Stir in the bread and let it soak for 8 to 10 minutes. Pour the bread mixture into the prepared baking dish. Place the baking dish into a pan that is a bit larger, with sides that come up to at least three-quarters of the height of the caramelized baking dish. Pour boiling water into the larger pan to come halfway up the sides of the caramelized baking dish. (This is called a bain-marie and helps the bread pudding cook evenly.)

Carefully place the two pans together in the oven and bake until the pudding is golden brown, puffed, and a little firm, 45 to 60 minutes. Let cool for a bit, then pool some of the cream sauce onto individual serving plates, spoon warm bread pudding onto the sauce, and serve.

CREMA DE VAINILLA Y RON / RUM AND VANILLA CREAM SAUCE

MAKES 3 CUPS

2   cups heavy cream
1   cup granulated sugar
1   vanilla bean, split in half lengthwise
½   cup dark rum

In a saucepan, combine the cream, sugar, and vanilla bean and cook over low heat until big bubbles appear on top, 20 to 30 minutes. Remove from the heat, then stir in the rum. Serve warm.

Guanábana is a tropical fruit also known as soursop. The unusual fruit is bright green with small, prickly bumps all over the outside; the flesh inside is creamy white, with rather large black seeds. The flavor is often described as a combination of pineapple and strawberry, and the texture as reminiscent of banana. Soursop's creaminess works wonderfully in these otherwise traditional Caribbean-style flans. The flans will need to chill in the refrigerator overnight, so plan ahead.

FLAN DE GUANÁBANA
Soursop Custard

SERVES 6

1 cup granulated sugar
½ cup peeled and seeded soursop pulp (from about 1 soursop)
1¾ cups sweetened condensed milk
½ cup whole milk
6 large eggs
1 tablespoon good-quality vanilla extract

Preheat the oven to 350°F.

In a saucepan, combine the sugar and ½ cup water and cook over medium-high heat, stirring often, until the sugar has dissolved completely. Reduce the heat to medium and cook until the syrup turns golden brown. Pour into six 6-ounce ramekins or custard cups and carefully tip them to coat the insides.

In a blender, combine the soursop pulp, condensed milk, whole milk, eggs, and vanilla and blend for about 45 seconds, until all of the ingredients are mixed well. Pour the mixture into the prepared ramekins and put them into a pan that is a bit larger, with sides that come up to at least three-quarters of the height of the ramekins. Pour boiling water into the larger pan to come halfway up the sides of the ramekins. (This is called a bain-marie and helps the custard cook evenly.)

Carefully place the pan in the oven and bake for about 1 hour, until a knife inserted into the custard comes out clean. Let cool to room temperature and refrigerate overnight. Unmold and serve cool.

This recipe is inspired by the Dulce de Tomate de Palo, a small variety of tomato grown in the Puerto Rican countryside. This was one of my grandmother's signature sweet dishes, and I ate it frequently when we visited her. As the years have come and gone, the recipe has evolved, taking on a Caprese twist, but my grandmother's spirit is always with me when I make this.

DULCE DE TOMATE SERVIDO CON HELADO DE QUESO DEL PAÍS Y ALBAHACA

Cherry Tomatoes in Syrup with Fresh Cheese and Basil Ice Cream

SERVES 6

32	cherry tomatoes
2	cups granulated sugar
2	cinnamon sticks
½	cup tomato paste
3	tablespoons red wine vinegar
2	vanilla beans, split in half lengthwise
	Fresh Cheese and Basil Ice Cream (recipe follows), for serving
	Pine nuts, toasted, for garnish
	Basil leaves, for garnish

Fill a large bowl with ice water and set aside. In a medium saucepan, bring 2 quarts water to a boil. Score the tomatoes with a little X on one end and drop them into the boiling water for 20 to 25 seconds. Drain and immediately plunge them into the ice water. From the stem end, peel a small piece of skin from one tomato. Squeeze gently and the skin should easily slide off the tomato. Peel all of the tomatoes.

In a medium saucepan, bring 6 cups water, the sugar, cinnamon sticks, tomato paste, vinegar, and vanilla beans to a boil. Simmer for 45 minutes, or until reduced to a thick syrup. Remove from the heat, put the tomatoes in the syrup, and let cool to room temperature. Cover and chill for at least 2 hours or store, covered, in the refrigerator for up to 2 weeks.

Put some of the tomatoes in the bottom of each dessert bowl and top with a scoop of ice cream. Sprinkle each serving with the pine nuts and basil.

HELADO DE QUESO DEL PAÍS Y ALBAHACA / FRESH CHEESE AND BASIL ICE CREAM

MAKES 6 TO 8 SERVINGS

2	cups heavy cream
½	cup whole milk
3	teaspoons chopped fresh basil
4	egg yolks
¼	cup granulated sugar
3	tablespoons simple syrup (page 235)
5	ounces crumbled queso del país (fresh white cheese)

Fill a large bowl with ice water and set aside.

Put the cream, milk, and 1 teaspoon of the basil in a saucepan. Bring to a boil, then immediately remove from the heat. Set aside.

In a medium bowl, beat together the egg yolks and sugar with an electric mixer until pale yellow in color and thickened. While mixing on low speed, slowly add some of the warm cream mixture to the egg mixture to temper the egg yolks. Transfer the egg mixture to the saucepan with the warm cream and cook over medium heat until thick enough to coat the back of a spoon, 2 to 3 minutes.

In a medium bowl, stir together the simple syrup and cheese. Add the egg and cream mixture to the cheese mixture and beat with a whisk until soft. Stir in the remaining 2 teaspoons basil, and set the mixture over the bowl of ice water to cool. Transfer to an ice cream machine and freeze according to the manufacturer's instructions. Transfer to an airtight container and freeze until ready to serve, but no longer than 2 weeks.

NOTE: For this recipe you can use ricotta instead of the *queso del país*.

You don't have to wait for morning to enjoy these doughnuts. In fact, for breakfast most Puerto Ricans would prefer a salty ham and egg sandwich on crusty bread to a sweet pastry. (Though that doesn't mean we won't also have a little dessert or midmorning snack following that breakfast sandwich.) Try these as an afternoon pick-me-up or as dessert after a casual supper. The simple sprinkling of cinnamon and sugar over these maple-scented fried doughnuts makes the perfect match for café con leche.

DONAS CON AZÚCAR Y CANELA
Doughnuts with Sugar and Cinnamon

MAKES 12

1½ cups milk
1   teaspoon maple syrup
⅓   cup vegetable shortening
1½ tablespoons instant yeast
⅓   cup warm water (100°F)
2   large eggs, beaten
1   cup sugar
1½ teaspoons kosher salt
4   cups all-purpose flour,
    plus more for dusting
    Vegetable oil, for deep-frying
¼   cup ground cinnamon

In a saucepan, heat the milk and maple syrup together over medium heat for 3 to 4 minutes. Put the shortening in the bowl of a stand mixer and pour the hot milk mixture over it.

In a small bowl, sprinkle the yeast over the warm water and allow it to stand until dissolved, about 5 minutes. Into the bowl of a stand mixer fitted with the paddle attachment, pour the yeast mixture with the shortening mixture, then add the eggs, ½ cup of the sugar, the salt, and 2 cups of the flour. Mix on low speed until the flour is just incorporated. Scrape down the sides of the bowl, add the remaining 2 cups flour, and mix again on low speed. Scrape down the sides, switch to the dough hook attachment of the mixer, and mix again until the dough becomes smooth and pulls away from the sides of the bowl, 4 to 5 minutes. Transfer to an oiled bowl, cover, and let rise until the dough has doubled in size, 45 minutes to 1 hour.

On a lightly floured surface, roll out the dough to ⅜ inch thick. Using a doughnut cutter, cut out rings, then cover them with a clean kitchen towel and let rise again for about 30 minutes.

In a deep fryer or large Dutch oven, heat the oil over medium-high heat to 350°F. Line a plate with paper towels. In a small bowl or plate, mix together the remaining ½ cup sugar and the cinnamon and set aside.

Carefully drop the doughnuts into the oil, being careful not to overcrowd the oil. Fry until golden brown, about 1 minute on each side. Remove from the oil and drain on the paper towel–lined plate. Dust each doughnut on both sides with the cinnamon-sugar and serve hot.

A beautiful cake to make for a special occasion, this jelly-roll-style confection has a spiral of yellow-orange passion fruit filling in the middle. The mascarpone icing that is spread over the cake is sprinkled with crunchy bits of meringue, giving the cake multiple textures and flavors. It's a beautiful cake when presented whole and even prettier when sliced.

BRAZO GITANO DE PARCHA
Passion Fruit Roulade

SERVES 6

FOR THE CAKE:
Butter, for the pan
5 eggs, separated
¼ teaspoon kosher salt
⅔ cup granulated sugar
1 cup cake flour
½ cup confectioners' sugar

FOR THE PASSION FRUIT FILLING:
2 cups milk
2 egg yolks
1 large egg
½ cup granulated sugar
1 cup cornstarch
2 tablespoons butter
¼ cup fresh passion fruit pulp
¼ cup undiluted passion fruit juice concentrate

FOR THE MASCARPONE FROSTING:
¾ cup heavy cream
8 ounces mascarpone cheese, at room temperature
1 teaspoon good-quality vanilla extract
1 teaspoon fresh lime juice
½ cup confectioners' sugar
½ cup crumbled store-bought crisp meringues, for garnish
Fresh passion fruit pulp, for garnish (optional)

MAKE THE CAKE: Preheat the oven to 400°F. Lightly butter the bottom and sides of a 10-by-15-inch jelly-roll pan and line it with parchment paper.

In the bowl of a stand mixer fitted with the paddle attachment, beat together the egg yolks, salt, 1 tablespoon water, and the granulated sugar until creamy and thick, about 2 minutes. Add the flour and beat until the flour is incorporated. In a separate bowl, beat the egg whites until stiff peaks form, then gently fold them into the yolk mixture. Pour the batter into the prepared pan and bake for 10 to 15 minutes, until golden brown. Let the cake cool in the pan for about 5 minutes.

On a sheet of waxed paper that is a bit bigger than the cake, sprinkle the confectioners' sugar to cover. Quickly turn the cake out onto the confectioners' sugar and let the cake cool completely before removing the parchment paper from the surface.

MAKE THE PASSION FRUIT FILLING: In a saucepan, bring the milk to a boil over medium-high heat. In a medium bowl, whisk together the egg yolks and the whole egg. Stir together the sugar and cornstarch and add to the egg mixture, mixing with an electric mixer until smooth and pale yellow in color. Drizzle the boiling milk into the bowl little by little while mixing on low speed to temper the eggs. Return the mixture to the saucepan and bring to a boil over medium-high heat, stirring continuously. When the mixture has thickened, remove from the heat and add the butter, passion fruit pulp, and passion fruit juice and mix well. Cover with plastic wrap and refrigerate until the filling has cooled to at least room temperature.

Spread the filling evenly over the surface of the cake, then carefully roll the cake into a spiral starting from one of the long ends. Cover and refrigerate until ready to frost and serve.

MAKE THE MASCARPONE FROSTING: In the bowl of a stand mixer fitted with the whisk attachment, whip the cream until stiff peaks form. In a separate bowl, mix together the cheese, vanilla, lime juice, and confectioners' sugar until smooth. Gently fold the whipped cream into the cheese mixture until completely incorporated.

Spread the frosting evenly over the cake with a metal icing spatula. Sprinkle the top with the crumbled meringues and passion fruit pulp, if you like. Slice and serve.

Cool, thick panna cotta made from tangy cream cheese and scented with vanilla is the perfect vehicle for this guava filling. Guavas are small green tropical fruits that have beautiful rose-colored flesh on the inside. The aroma is citrusy and the flavor similar to a strawberry—it's perfect with the panna cotta's creamy texture.

PANNA COTTA DE QUESO CREMA Y VAINILLA RELLENA DE GUAYABA
Cream Cheese and Vanilla Panna Cotta with Guava Filling

SERVES 6

FOR THE PANNA COTTA:
- 1 tablespoon unflavored gelatin powder
- 1 cup plus 2 tablespoons milk
- 1 cup plus 2 tablespoons heavy cream
- 1 vanilla bean, split in half lengthwise, seeds scraped out (reserve both)
- 3 tablespoons granulated sugar
- 1 ounce cream cheese, softened

FOR THE GUAVA FILLING:
- 1 (7-ounce) can or jar of guava shells in heavy syrup (available online or in the international section of the supermarket)
- ½ cup fresh lemon juice

MAKE THE PANNA COTTA: Sprinkle the gelatin over ¼ cup cold water and let stand until softened, about 5 minutes. In a medium saucepan, combine the milk, cream, vanilla bean pod and seeds, sugar, and cream cheese and bring to a simmer over medium-low heat. Remove the vanilla bean pod and discard it or save for another use. Add the dissolved gelatin to the saucepan and remove from the heat. Stir until the mixture is smooth. Fill six 4-ounce silicone hemisphere (or other shape) molds halfway with the panna cotta mixture, and freeze until the mixture is set.

MAKE THE GUAVA FILLING: In a blender, combine the guava and lemon juice and blend until smooth. Pour into six 1½-ounce molds and freeze until set.

Remove the frozen guava from the molds and place them in the molds with the panna cotta; pour the rest of the panna cotta mixture on top. Freeze until set. Before serving, place the molds in the refrigerator for about 4 hours to soften the frozen guava inside.

NOTE: You'll need two sizes of silicone molds for this restaurant-style dessert: 4-ounce molds (we use hemisphere molds) for the panna cotta, and 1½-ounce ones for the guava filling, which is frozen separately and then added to the half-full panna cotta molds and covered with more panna cotta.

Maví is a liquid ingredient made from the bark of a tree that grows in Puerto Rico and other tropical places. Soaked in water, with sugar, ginger, and cinnamon, the bark releases a pleasant, slightly bitter, tannic flavor. The concentrate can then be mixed with soda water to make a fizzy drink or left to ferment, making it slightly stronger. It's a nice complement to the rum and watermelon in this granita. The homemade *maví* will take about three days to ferment, so plan ahead. Alternatively, use readymade *maví*, available online and at international markets.

PIRAGUA DE MAVÍ, RON Y SANDÍA
Granita of Mauby, Rum and Watermelon

SERVES 6

FOR THE GRANITA:
- 2 cups Mauby (recipe follows) or prepared mavi (available online)
- ½ cup granulated sugar
- ½ cup fresh lime juice
- ½ cup light rum
- 4 cups seeded and diced watermelon

FOR THE VANILLA AND RUM WHIPPED CREAM:
- 1 cup heavy cream
- 2 tablespoons granulated sugar
- 1 tablespoon good-quality vanilla extract
- ⅓ cup white rum

MAKE THE GRANITA: In a medium saucepan, combine the mauby and sugar and cook over medium heat until the sugar has dissolved completely. Let cool completely, then add the lime juice, rum, and diced watermelon. Pour into a glass or stainless-steel dish that is about 9 by 13 inches and at least 2 inches deep. Freeze until the granita becomes slushy, about 2 hours. Once it is slushy, remove and scrape the entire mixture with a fork to make a grainy texture—like a coarse slushy. Return to the freezer and repeat the scraping process every hour until the granita is completely frozen.

MAKE THE VANILLA AND RUM WHIPPED CREAM: Put the heavy cream in the bowl of a stand mixer fitted with the whisk attachment. Whip on high speed for 1 minute, then gradually add the sugar while continuing to mix. When soft peaks have formed, add the vanilla and rum and continue to whisk on high speed until stiff peaks form. Store any unused portion in an airtight container for up to 3 hours.

When the granita is fully frozen, use an ice cream scoop or large spoon to divide it among individual wineglasses or dessert dishes. Garnish with a dollop of the whipped cream and serve immediately.

MAVÍ / MAUBY

MAKES 1 GALLON

- 1 ounce (2 tablespoons) mauby tree bark (available online)
- 4 (1-inch-long) slices peeled fresh ginger
- 1 cinnamon stick
- 2½ cups granulated sugar
- 2½ cups light brown sugar

In a medium saucepan, combine the mauby tree bark, ginger, cinnamon stick, and 1½ cups water. Bring to a boil over high heat, then reduce the heat to medium, cover, and cook for 5 minutes. Strain the maví through a fine-mesh sieve set over a bowl and let cool completely.

In a large bowl, combine the granulated sugar, brown sugar, and 12 cups water. Add 2 cups of the cooled maví and mix well. Strain through a sieve lined with cheesecloth into a bowl, then return to the bowl. Beat the mixture until it becomes foamy. Pour into a glass bottle, filling it three-quarters full, and place a paper in the shape of a loose cone on top of the bottle. (Never cover the bottle tightly.) Let it stand for 3 to 4 days at room temperature (preferably in a sunny spot) to allow the mauby to ferment. Refrigerate uncovered and serve chilled.

Named for the Spanish island of Mallorca, these lovely round breads resemble a rosette that has been dusted with snow. Most Puerto Ricans purchase mallorcas from the Spanish-style panaderías on the island. But if you aren't lucky enough to live close to a panadería, it is possible to make these breads at home with just a little practice.

The breads are a bit crunchy on the outside and give way to a moist, pillowy interior. In this recipe, I use both butter and olive oil. The butter helps the dough form the brown crust and interior layers while the olive oil provides the little bit of heaviness needed to keep the dough moist and lends a hint of Spanish flavor. Once baked, sprinkle them with powdered sugar if you like and enjoy with coffee, or slice them in halves to make a ham-and-cheese pressed sandwich.

PAN DE MALLORCA
Mallorca Bread

MAKES 12 BUNS

1 cup milk
2¼ teaspoons instant yeast
7 large egg yolks
¾ cup granulated sugar
1 cup (2 sticks) unsalted butter, melted
6 tablespoons olive oil
6 cups all-purpose flour, plus more for dusting
2 cups confectioners' sugar

In a small saucepan set over medium heat, combine the milk and 1 cup water and heat until warm to the touch but not yet steaming. Transfer the warm liquid to a large bowl and sprinkle the yeast on top; allow it to sit for 2 to 3 minutes. In another bowl, combine the egg yolks, sugar, ½ cup of the melted butter, and 3 tablespoons of the oil and whisk well. Pour the yeast mixture into the egg mixture and whisk to combine. Add the flour, mixing with a wooden spoon or spatula until just combined. Cover with plastic wrap and let sit in a warm place until the dough doubles in size. Transfer to the refrigerator and chill for at least 3 hours or up to overnight.

Line a baking sheet with parchment paper. Turn the dough out onto a floured surface and divide the dough into 12 equal pieces. Using your hands, roll them into rope shapes that are about 12 inches long. Brush the ropes with some of the remaining butter and oil and roll up tightly from one end to the other. Tuck in the ends and brush the top with butter and oil. Place the dough rolls on the prepared baking sheet and cover. Set aside until doubled in size, about 45 minutes.

Preheat the oven to 350°F.

Bake the rolls until the tops are golden brown, 20 to 25 minutes. While still warm, dust generously with confectioners' sugar. Serve warm or at room temperature.

PANADERÍAS

Our traditional bakeries, found all over the island, are not just a place to buy bread; they are cafés, grocery stores, and gathering places all at once.

In major cities, you will find *panaderías* that are very large, with tables and waitresses to take your order—pastries and sandwiches, and often also appetizers and special plated meals. *Pan de agua,* or water bread, is a basic white bread that is perfect for Puerto Rican meat and cheese sandwiches. The crisp, light brown crust shatters easily, giving way to the pillowy soft interior. When toasted in a press with a filling of ham, roast pork, Swiss cheese, and pickles, this becomes the famous Cubano sandwich. Or, if you swap the bread out for a sweet yellow roll, you have the Media Noche. (One sandwich sensation on the island has come from the tiny kitchens of mobile food trucks that specialize in the Tripleta, which combines three types of meat, usually chicken, pork, and beef.)

The *panadería* also serves as a source where home cooks can buy specialty ingredients such as imported Spanish goods—like olives, anchovies, and cured hams—as well as preserved sweets, jellies, and candies. In the mornings, long lines of customers will snake past the pastry cases. Folks grabbing a morning café con leche (equal parts espresso and steamed milk); a ham, egg, and cheese sandwich; or a *mallorca* (page 228) or other pastry make this a morning ritual. Throughout the day people stop in for a quick lunch, gather for business meetings, or bump into friends while they wait for their order. The *panadería* is a special part of the social fabric that makes up life in Puerto Rico.

CÓCTELES

Cocktails

SIMPLE SYRUP

MAKES ABOUT ½ CUP

½ cup sugar (preferably Demerara)

In a small saucepan, heat the sugar and ½ cup water over medium-high heat, stirring, until the sugar has completely dissolved. Let cool, then cover and keep in the refrigerator for up to 1 month.

CINNAMON SYRUP
To make cinnamon-infused simple syrup, place 2 cinnamon sticks in a clean jar or small bowl and pour the warm simple syrup over them. Let cool to room temperature and use immediately or remove the cinnamon sticks, cover, and keep in the refrigerator for up to 1 month.

MINT SYRUP
Bruise 8 fresh mint leaves by gently crushing or smacking them between your palms; put them in a clean jar. Before chilling the syrup, but after it has come to room temperature, pour the syrup over the mint. Let stand at room temperature for at least 1 hour or cover and chill for up to 1 day, then remove the leaves and keep in the refrigerator for up to 1 month.

AJÍ DULCE SYRUP
The small, sweet peppers known in Puerto Rico as ají dulce look like habañeros but are not hot. If you can't find ají dulce peppers, you can substitute any small, sweet red peppers. While the simple syrup is still warm, pour it over 2 ají dulce peppers. Let cool to room temperature, then strain the syrup into a clean jar and discard the peppers. Use immediately or cover and keep in the refrigerator for up to 1 month.

CÓCTEL LIBRE

This recipe is more refreshing and lighter than a Cuba Libre because it contains no cola. The bitters in this drink take their botanical hints from coffee, chocolate, red chiles, and ginger—all alleged aphrodisiacs. At the Santaella bar, we like to make large ice spheres (you can buy these molds online) out of fresh coconut water. They not only keep drinks well chilled but also add subtle flavor.

SERVES 1

½ fluid ounce (1 tablespoon) simple syrup (opposite)
½ fluid ounce (1 tablespoon) fresh coconut water
3 dashes Dr. Adam Elmegirab's Aphrodite Bitters
2 fluid ounces (¼ cup) dark aged rum
1 large fresh coconut water ice sphere

In a small glass pitcher, stir together the simple syrup, coconut water, bitters, and rum and strain into a rocks glass over the coconut water ice sphere.

RON EMBRUJADO

In this twist on the classic rum and Coke, the rum is *embrujado* ("haunted") by the mysterious flavors of our homemade tamarind cola.

SERVES 1

2   fluid ounces (¼ cup) aged rum
6   fluid ounces (¾ cup) Tamarind Housemade Cola (recipe follows)

Fill a highball glass with ice. Pour the rum into the bottom of the glass, then begin filling the glass with the cola. Stop about halfway, give it a quick stir, and add more soda, leaving about 1 inch of space at the top of the glass. Stir again and serve immediately.

HOUSEMADE TAMARIND COLA

MAKES 3 CUPS (24 FLUID OUNCES)

12   fluid ounces (1½ cups) tamarind juice concentrate (available online)
2   teaspoons fresh lemon juice
2   teaspoons fresh lime juice
¾   fluid ounce (1½ tablespoons) cinnamon-infused simple syrup (page 235)
½   fluid ounce (1 tablespoon) Godiva chocolate liqueur

Pour the tamarind juice concentrate, lemon and lime juices, simple syrup, and liqueur into a soda siphon. Charge it twice and let it sit overnight in the refrigerator. Give it a hard shake and it's ready to serve.

PUERTO RICAN RUM

It is likely that rum is the most recognized product that Puerto Rico produces. Sugar cane, which is mashed, cooked down into molasses, fermented, and distilled to make rum, has been grown on our island, as in much of the Caribbean, since the early 1500s. Molasses and rum were valuable exports that were carried across vast distances among the Caribbean colonies, Europe, and Africa in a system known as the Triangular Trade, a profitable but inhumane system based on slave labor. The very humans that helped grow and harvest the cane and produce the rum and molasses were considered a product themselves. Slavery ended, but the thirst for rum did not, and now Puerto Rico proudly produces 80 percent of all of the rum that is purchased in America.

Great care is taken throughout the fermentation, distillation, aging, and bottling process. Puerto Rican rum is aged in barrels made from American white oak. The rum designated white or silver label is very light in color. Gold refers to a rum that has been in the barrel from one to four years, and amber or a dark label indicates rum that has been aged for more than four years. Most Puerto Rican rum producers buy used oak barrels that have been previously used to age whiskey. The origin of the barrels along with the aging times contribute to their distinct attributes. During the aging process, master blenders will take samples from the barrels and evaluate them for taste, color, and aroma.

Puerto Rico is home to very large producers like Bacardi and Don Q as well as small-batch, traditional producers like Ron del Barrilito. The industry has provided thousands of jobs to Puerto Ricans and contributed billions of dollars to the economy. Rum is not just a delicious spirit to us—it is an important part of our history and livelihood.

There is also a tradition of making "moonshine" rum, called *pitorro*, and sharing it with friends and family. You might be at a party and someone will pull out a bottle or jar of very strong, crystal-clear homemade spirit. It becomes much more palatable if infused with flavorings such as dried fruit, cinnamon, and vanilla bean—*ron perfumado*. Be careful when eating the liquor-soaked fruit: The natural sugars intensify the alcohol, and it's easy to consume too much. You may choose to indulge in a swig of moonshine if the opportunity arises, but be warned: if not distilled correctly, it can be harmful, and in any case, it's still illegal!

VERANO SIN FIN

Falernum, a syrup typically used in tropical-style drinks, gives this rum and fruit juice cocktail complexity. It is a festive drink promising an endless summer (*verano sin fin*), served in a large hurricane glass and, in the spirit of the island, with a pretty, fresh pineapple garnish.

SERVES 1

½ cup diced peeled pineapple
¾ fluid ounce (1½ tablespoons) fresh lime juice
¾ fluid ounce (1½ tablespoons) simple syrup (page 235)
½ fluid ounce (1 tablespoon) falernum (recipe follows)
2 fluid ounces (¼ cup) light rum
Pineapple leaves and pineapple slices or spears, for garnish

In a mixing glass, muddle the diced pineapple, lime juice, and simple syrup, then pour in the falernum and rum. Pour the mixture into a shaker over ice and give it a few hard shakes. Strain over fresh ice into a hurricane or other large cocktail glass. Garnish with pineapple leaves and fresh pineapple slices and serve.

FALERNUM

MAKES 3 CUPS

2 tablespoons freshly grated nutmeg
1 tablespoon ground allspice
35 whole cloves
8 fluid ounces (1 cup) rum
Zest of 8 lemons
½ cup grated peeled fresh ginger (from about ⅓ pound ginger)
2 cups granulated sugar
½ cup sliced almonds
½ teaspoon pure almond extract

In a small, dry skillet, cook the nutmeg, allspice, and cloves over medium heat until their aromas intensify, about 5 minutes. In a clean jar or bottle with a lid, combine the rum, lemon zest, and ginger. Seal the container and let it sit overnight at room temperature to infuse.

Bring the sugar and 1 cup water to a boil in a small saucepan and cook, stirring, until the sugar has dissolved completely. Remove from the heat and stir in the almonds and almond extract. Let cool completely, then add to the rum mixture and stir well. Cover and keep refrigerated until ready to use, but no longer than 3 weeks.

JULEP DE MANGÓ

This is our tropical version of a mint julep. Instead of bourbon, we use dark rum, but the infusion of mint and the coldness of the crushed ice is the same. Serve in a sparkling-silver julep cup to keep it super-cold.

SERVES 1

¾ fluid ounce (1½ tablespoons) mango puree, plus more for garnish
2   tablespoons raw (Demerara) sugar
¼ fluid ounce (½ tablespoon) mint simple syrup (page 235)
5   fresh mint leaves
½ fluid ounce (1 tablespoon) fresh lemon/lime juice
     Crushed ice
1½ fluid ounces (3 tablespoons) dark aged rum

In a julep glass, put the mango puree, 1 tablespoon of the raw sugar, the simple syrup, 4 of the mint leaves and juice. Muddle lightly with a bit of crushed ice while pouring in the rum. Top off with more crushed ice and garnish with the remaining mint leaf and a little mango puree.

EL MERCADO

Santaella sits just across from one of the oldest and most beautiful markets in the city. Santurce Market is a large, regal building with large doors on all sides that open to make it a beautiful open-air market with many vendor stalls inside selling all types of local produce. El Mercado (pictured at right) is a drink that pays homage to all the beautiful markets we love.

SERVES 2

4   fluid ounces (½ cup) fresh papaya pulp
½ fluid ounce (1 tablespoon) fresh lemon juice
½ fluid ounce (1 tablespoon) simple syrup (page 235)
½ fluid ounce (1 tablespoon) orange curaçao
¼ fluid ounce (½ tablespoon) cinnamon simple syrup (page 235)
2   ounces (¼ cup) Puerto Rican white rum
     Dash of Angostura bitters
2   fresh lime wheels, for garnish
2   fresh papaya spears, for garnish

In a mixing glass or shaker, combine the papaya, lemon juice, simple syrup, curaçao, cinnamon-infused simple syrup, rum, and bitters; add ice and shake hard. Strain into two classic cocktail glasses. Garnish with the lime and papaya and serve.

JIBARITO MULE

A Moscow Mule—or, here, a Jibarito Mule—is one of the most refreshing cockails there is. We love the cold copper of a mule cup against our hands in this tropical paradise. It creates a nice touch sensation to go with the taste.

SERVES 1

½   fluid ounce (1 tablespoon) fresh lemon/lime juice
½   fluid ounce (1 tablespoon) pique (page 61)
1½ fluid ounces (3 tablespoons) spiced rum
¾   fluid ounce (1½ tablespoons) homemade ginger
     beer (recipe follows)
     Lime slices, for garnish
     Fresh oregano sprig, for garnish

In a shaker, combine the lemon/lime juice, pique infusion, and rum and shake with ice until well mixed. Pour into a copper mule cup over fresh ice and top off with the ginger beer. Garnish with a lime slice and sprig of oregano.

GINGER BEER

MAKES ABOUT 3 CUPS

1   pound fresh ginger, peeled and grated
     (1 to ½ cups)
½   cup sugar
2   (1-inch long) strips orange peel
4   (1-inch long) strips lemon peel
1   cup freshly squeezed lemon juice
2½ teaspoons active dry yeast

In a large saucepan, combine 6 cups water with the ginger, sugar, orange and lemon peels, and lemon juice. Bring to a boil over medium heat. Cook for about 5 minutes; remove from the heat and let cool until lukewarm.

Add the yeast and stir until well incorporated. Pour the mixture into a glass bottle, screw on the cap or wedge a cork into the top, shake once and let it sit at room temperature for around 48 hours. Open the bottle (being careful to point the cap or cork away from your face as pressure can build up inside the bottle) and check if it has reached the desired level of effervescence. Once it is bubbly to your liking, refrigerate the bottle. The beer will keep in the refrigerator for at least 2 weeks, but it is a good idea to open the bottle once a day to release excess bubbles.

COQUITO

Creamy *coquito* is a very old-fashioned drink we enjoy at Christmastime. Though it has no eggs, you might think of it as a tropical version of eggnog since it has a similarly dense, velvety consistency along with a comforting fragrance. Laced with rich, dark Puerto Rican rum, this drink warms up any holiday party.

SERVES 6 TO 8

3   cups fresh coconut milk (page 187)
1   (14-ounce) can sweetened condensed milk
1   (15-ounce) can cream of coconut
½   teaspoon ground cinnamon, plus more for garnish
¼   teaspoon freshly ground nutmeg
2   cups Puerto Rican dark rum

Combine the coconut milk, sweetened condensed milk, cream of coconut, cinnamon, nutmeg, and rum in a blender and process on high speed until the mixture is foamy, about 2 minutes. Pour the coquito into a clean glass bottle or pitcher and chill in the refrigerator for at least an hour. (It will keep, refrigerated, for at least 3 weeks.) To serve, pour into individual glasses and garnish with more cinnamon.

SANTA GUANÁBANA

Guanábana, or soursop, is an interesting fruit that has green spiny skin and a creamy, strawberry-banana-flavored flesh (see page 209). Mixed with light rum and a little hit of fresh basil and served in a coupe, it makes an elegant drink (pictured at right).

SERVES 1

2   fluid ounces (4 tablespoons) seeded fresh soursop pulp
½   fluid ounce (1 tablespoon) simple syrup (page 235)
5   medium fresh basil leaves
1½   teaspoons fresh lemon juice
1½   teaspoons fresh lime juice
2   fluid ounces (¼ cup) Puerto Rican light rum
     Dark chocolate dust (finely grated dark chocolate)

In a blender, combine the soursop pulp, simple syrup, basil, and juices, and blend until the mixture is light green and smooth. Pour into a shaker filled halfway with ice, add the rum and shake well. Strain into a classic cut-glass Champagne coupe or a cocktail glass, top with dark chocolate dust, and serve.

CLASSIC MOJITO

Originally from our neighbors on the island of Cuba, the mojito is now ubiquitous on all of the tropical islands. The act of "muddling" or agitating the mint, sugar, and citrus juices together helps dissolve the sugar while extracting intense flavor from the mint. The result is one of the most refreshing cocktails in the world.

SERVES 2

2   tablespoons fresh lemon juice
2   tablespoons fresh lime juice
4   teaspoons of sugar
16 fresh mint leaves, plus more for garnish
½   cup light Puerto Rican rum
2   cups crushed ice
¼   cup club soda
    Lime slices, for garnish

In the bottom of a cocktail shaker or a pint glass, place the lemon and lime juice, sugar, and mint leaves. Muddle using a wooden spoon or cocktail muddler until the sugar has dissolved and the mint is bruised. Add the rum, stir, and pour into two highball glasses filled with ice. Top off with the club soda and garnish with the mint leaves and lime slice.

PUERTO RICAN BLOODY MARY

Nothing cures a Sunday morning hangover better than a Bloody Mary. Drink one with the Huevos Revueltos con Longaniza (page 108) for a tropical brunch and you will be back to normal in no time. Since this recipe (pictured at left) calls for letting the mixture chill overnight for the flavors to marry, it's an ideal make-ahead drink for a gathering.

SERVES 8

3   cups tomato juice
2   tablespoons fresh lemon juice
2   tablespoons fresh lime juice
1   tablespoon Worcestershire sauce
2   tablespoons peeled and grated fresh horseradish
1½   tablespoons kosher salt
1   teaspoon Puerto Rican pique (page 61)
1   teaspoon celery salt
¾   teaspoon freshly ground black pepper
1   tablespoon minced fresh cilantro
1   tablespoon seeded and minced ajíes dulces (page 41)
2   cups light Puerto Rican rum
8   celery stalks, for garnish
     Dill pickle spears, for garnish
     Ajíes dulces, for garnish
     Olives, for garnish

In a blender place all the ingredients except the rum and garnishes. Mix for about 1 minute, until completely combined. Cover and refrigerate overnight. Fill highball glasses halfway with ice. Into each pour 2 ounces of the rum and 4 ounces of the blended mix, stirring well until combined. Garnish with the celery stalks, dill pickle, ajíes dulces, and olives. Serve immediately.

ACKNOWLEDGMENTS

I would like to offer my sincerest gratitude to the following, all of whom had some important role in putting this book together:

My mother, Carmen Laura Betancourt, for giving her love and examples, for teaching me responsibility and perseverance

My father, Jose "Caguita" Santaella, for being the one who first showed me a love for this industry

My sister, "Cuca," and my brother, Antonio Luis, for their love and support

Kristian Toro (pictured, below), for your extraordinary mind and vision, for pushing me and Santaella to the next level, and for being part of my life

Ivan Benitez (pictured, above left), for being my right hand—and my left— and having the patience to deal with me for so many years

Sofia Tirado (pictured, above right), for your great friendship—this book would not have been possible without you

Ben Fink, for your impeccable photography skills and advice

Christopher Steighner, for believing in me and my work, for being so kind and a brilliant editor

Angie Mosier (pictured, center), for your lovely writing and for letting yourself become a Puerto Rican through this book

Eric Ripert, for your friendship of many years, for being one of my biggest inspirations, and for writing a great foreword

Gary Danko, for being one of the best teachers I could have

Ferran Adriá, for your support and the opportunity of being able to work with you

Alfredo Ayala, for your mentorship

Blair Richardson

Antonio Garcia Padilla

Popular, Inc.

Richard and Conxita Carrion, for your loyalty throughout the years

Luisita Rangel de Ferré and her daughters Maria Luisa, Maria Eugenia, and Loren

Kenneth Martinez, for helping me develop the recipes

Anais Melero and "Pepe" Carballido

Department of Economic Development & Commerce of Puerto Rico

Puerto Rico Tourism Company

Ryan Dickie

Enrique Villa del Corral

Eduardo Santiago

Angel Collado Schwartz

Laura Guerra

Ignacio "Nacho" Lopez

Rafael Jimenez

Gamaliel de la Mata

And the wonderful staff of Santaella restaurant, including the kitchen staff, waiters, and bartenders.

CONVERSION CHART

LIQUID CONVERSIONS

U.S.	METRIC
1 tsp	5 ml
1 tbs	15 ml
2 tbs	30 ml
3 tbs	45 ml
¼ cup	60 ml
⅓ cup	75 ml
⅓ cup + 1 tbs	90 ml
⅓ cup + 2 tbs	100 ml
½ cup	120 ml
⅔ cup	150 ml
¾ cup	180 ml
¾ cup + 2 tbs	200 ml
1 cup	240 ml
1 cup + 2tbs	275 ml
1 ¼ cups	300 ml
1 ⅓ cups	325 ml
1 ½ cups	350 ml
1 ⅔ cups	375 ml
1 ¾ cups	400 ml
1 ¾ cups + 2 tbs	450 ml
2 cups (1 pint)	475 ml
2 ½ cups	600 ml
3 cups	720 ml
4 cups (1 quart)	945 ml
	(1,000 ml is 1 liter)

WEIGHT CONVERSIONS

U.S./U.K.	METRIC
½ oz	14 g
1 oz	28 g
1 ½ oz	43 g
2 oz	57 g
2 ½ oz	71 g
3 oz	85 g
3 ½ oz	100 g
4 oz	113 g
5 oz	142 g
6 oz	170 g
7 oz	200 g
8 oz	227 g
9 oz	255 g
10 oz	284 g
11 oz	312 g
12 oz	340 g
13 oz	368 g
14 oz	400 g
15 oz	425 g
1 lb	454 g

OVEN TEMPERATURES

°F	GAS MARK	°C
250	½	120
275	1	140
300	2	150
325	3	165
350	4	180
375	5	190
400	6	200
425	7	220
450	8	230
475	9	240
500	10	260
550	Broil	290

INDEX

Page references in italic refer to illustrations.